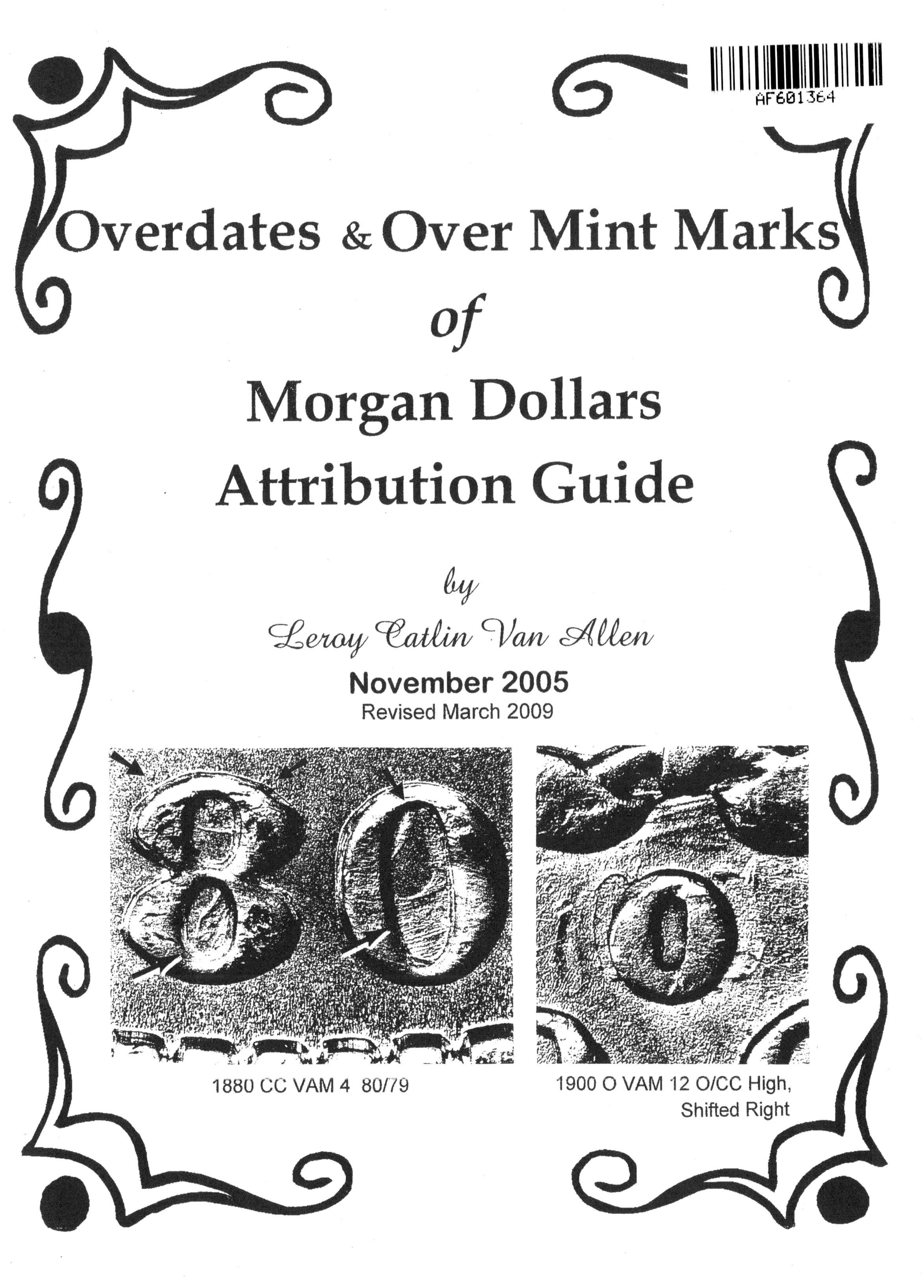

1880 CC VAM 4 80/79

1900 O VAM 12 O/CC High, Shifted Right

Published by

Rare Coin Investments (RCI)
P.O. Box C
Ironia, NJ 07845

Authors: Leroy C. Van Allen
Edited by: Michael S. Fey, Ph.D.

ISBN-13 number: 979-8-9919648-6-9

Printed in the United States

TABLE OF CONTENTS

LIST OF FIGURES

OVERDATES & OVER MINT MARKS OF MORGAN DOLLARS ATTRIBUTION GUIDE

INTRODUCTION

The Morgan dollar has **two years** with known **overdates** and also **two years** with known **over mint marks.** Overdates are a date digit punched over a different digit in a working die, usually the last one or two right digits. The Philadelphia Mint prepared the working dies for all of the mints that struck the Morgan dollar. Overdates were the result of salvaging the obverse working dies left over from one year by punching in the following years digit(s) so the expensive working dies could be utilized. The two overdate years known for the Morgan dollar are the **1880** with over **two dozen** different overdate dies of **8/7, 0/9 & 80/79** identified for the Philadelphia, Carson City, New Orleans and San Francisco struck coins and the **1887** with one **7/6** overdate identified for each of the Philadelphia and New Orleans Mints struck coins.

Similarly, over mint marks are one mint mark letter punched over a different mint mark letter(s) to salvage a reverse working die for use at a mint other than the one originally intended. This occurred in **1882** for the Morgan dollar when **three** reverse working dies with an S mint mark were re-punched with an **O over the S** and again in **1900** for **five** reverse working dies with a CC mint mark re-punched with an **O over the CC.**

Both the overdates and over mint marks can command substantial premium prices depending upon the extent of the underlying original digit or letter showing and their rarity. Also, some of the overdate and over mint mark underlying remains are quite faint and can be controversial as to their existence. One of the objectives of this report is to provide substantiation for each of these varieties through detailed discussions and photographs.

Separate sections treat the 1880 and 1887 overdates and the 1882 and 1900 over mint marks.

This update adds a number of new die combination varieties and some clashed die letter sub-varieties. For the **1880 P**, a new die combination of VAM 53 was reported by John Roberts in November 2008 that has the same obverse die as the VAM 29A 8/7 checkmark and clashed dies but with a new listed reverse die. The VAM 29A was reported by Joseph Wilson in May 2008 and has clashed dies with an incuse n at the Liberty head neck. A new clashed letters st at the lower right hair vee was reported for VAM 2/11 by Mark Kimpton in May 2004. Also, the 1880 P VAM 25 0/9 was de-listed as an overdate since the evidence of the 9 on the 0 is so weak and unconvincing. It is now only listed as a doubled date.

For the **1880 CC,** a new clashed letter n was reported for VAM 7A by Phil Perdue in May 2006.

A new die combination was listed for the **1880 O** of VAM 63 reported by Clayton Christiansen in March 2006. It combines the same 8/7 checkmark obverse die of VAMs 17 & 17 with a different reverse die with a medium oval O mint mark set high. Also, a new sub-variety of VAM 6D was reported by Laurence Galbraith in December 2007 that combines the 8/7 spike clashed die n and st obverse of VAMs 6A and 6B/49 with an unclashed VAM 6C reverse die.

All of the previously listed die varieties of 1882 O/S, 1887 7/6 and 1900 O/CC overdates and over mint marks have been found to be **valid** and have been **retained**. For the **1880 P** overdates, the **VAM 2** has been **eliminated** since it was determined to have the same dies as VAM 11 which was reported before VAM 2 and the VAM 11 had a more comprehensive description and is retained. However, the designation of **VAM 2/11** can also be used since the VAM 2 was listed and in use since 1973. **VAM 25** has been **de-listed** as an overdate because the evidence of being an 0/9 overdate is too weak and is now only listed as a doubled date. **VAM 10** remains a **possible** but not conclusive overdate. For the **1880 CC**, the **VAM 10** has been **de-listed** as an overdate since it has been shown that it is not a polished down VAM 5 as originally thought, but is only a dash and doubled 8 variety. The

1880 S VAM 11 0/9 overdate remains **controversial** as an overdate because of the strange looking polished remains inside the 0. However, these remains are similar to that of the well-known 1880 CC VAM 4 80/79 and simulation of the punching of digits into clay and the photo overlays makes a strong case that it is an 0/9 overdate.

Medal Room, Philadelphia Mint, 1901
George Morgan wielding mallet with dies and medals, age 56
(Report of The Director of The Mint, 1902)

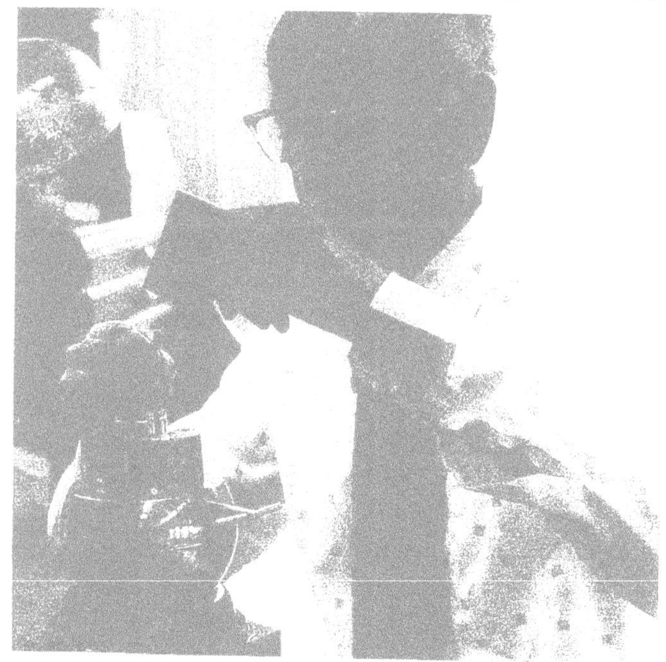

Punching Mint Mark Into Die, 1970s

Mint Mark Punches & Specimen Pieces, 1970s

HOW THE OVERDATES & OVER MINT MARKS WERE CREATED

For the 1880/79 overdates, only the right digit 8 in the date had been removed from the 1878 master hub to prepare the 1879 master hub for 1879. Each 1879 working die had only the last 9 digit punched by hand into it using a single digit punch. Thus, the **depth** of the last right **9 digit** on the original 1879 working dies **varied** compared to the 188 digits. This could have caused differences in the amounts of the underlying 7 and 9 remains after the 80 was punched in and the die polished because of the varying depths of the 9 in the die, since it was individually punched. Also, punching in the overdate digits of 80 could have been made with a two digit logotype or individual digit punches. This would have also caused **variations** in the **8 and 0 digit depths** and **positions** if the **single digit punch** was used for the overdate modification.

The author witnessed the die manufacturing process, including the punching of a mint mark into an Eisenhower die, during a tour of the Philadelphia Mint in 1978. The process of punching the date digits into the Morgan dollar working dies would have been similar. An accompanying photograph shows a mint worker punching the mint mark into an Eisenhower die. The dies were individually clamped into a jeweler's vise with the die in a vertical position, die face at the top and the design in the normal upright position. The mint mark punch was held in the right hand in a vertical position and carefully lowered against the die face and lined up in position by eye. **Three quick taps** within less than a second were given to the punch using a double headed 12 ounce mallet. A quick visual inspection with the naked eye was given to the mint mark to determine if it was of deep enough impression and of proper placement and orientation.

Some mint mark punches used in the 1970s are shown in the accompanying photograph and would have been similar to the individual date punches used on the Morgan dollar working dies.

The overdates and over mint marks of the Morgan dollar show **varying amounts** and **positions** of the remaining **underlying digits and letters**, as explained above. Modification of the working dies was performed using a mallet striking hand punches of digits and letters which resulted in the differences in the position of the overlying punched digits and letters and the depth of the punch. Subsequent basining and polishing of the working dies to prepare the die face with the correct curvature and smoothness would have removed the underlying digits or letters to **varying degrees**. This resulted in **strong** over dates and over mint marks showing as well as partial and **weak** ones with **different** positions.

The original date digits and mint marks were not ground off the working dies because this would have resulted in depressions on the dies and raised area in the normally flat fields of the coins. The digit and letter cavities in the working dies were also not filled up by welding because the electric arc and oxyacetylene welding techniques had not yet been invented in 1880. Instead, the hand punching of digits and letters into the working dies had to be used. The plastic metal flow during this punching was three dimensional since the digits and letters had depth plus width and height. It was a **complex metal flow** because of the design differences of the underlying and over struck numerals or letters. The second digit punch would have forced metal into the original die cavity as well as displaced the metal in the field. There are examples of the 1882 O/S and 1900 O/CC over mintmarks of the metal forced into the original letter cavity eventually **chipping back out** as the dies were used to strike coins. Some **distortion** and **closing** of the original die cavity also resulted from the plastic metal flow.

Later sections of this report show the **simulation** of the **plastic metal flow** in the dies by using **wooden date digits** and **letters** forced into **modeling clay**. The resulting positive wax casts show many of the features of actual over date and over mint mark features on the coins. The method of creating overdates on Morgan dollars by striking hand punches over existing digits in the working dies was simulated using wooden models of date digits punched into modeling clay and was presented in articles by the author in *Coin World Collectors' Clearinghouse* October 27 and November 3, 1976 issues.

1880 OVERDATES QUICK ATTRIBUTION SUMMARY

Because there are over **two dozen** known overdate varieties for the year 1880 of the Morgan dollar, a separate **quick attribution summary** is presented in the following pages. This should help in the quick identification of some of the weaker appearing and lesser known 1880 overdate varieties. The following chart summarizes the known overdate die varieties for the 1880 Philadelphia, Carson City, New Orleans and San Francisco Mints struck Morgan dollars.

The overdate die varieties are listed as a **VAM number** with the acronym **VAM** taken from the first letters of Van Allen and Mallis who co-authored the book, *Comprehensive Catalog & Encyclopedia of Morgan & Peace Dollars,* by Leroy C. Van Allen & A. George Mallis, DLRC Press, 3rd ed. 1992 & 4th ed. printing 1998. This is followed by the overdate title or name given to the variety. Next, it is designated as a **Top 100** or **Hot 50** variety if it is listed in the books, *The Top 100 Morgan Dollar Varieties: The VAM Keys* by Michael Fey & Jeff Oxman, 1996 and *SSDC Official Guide to the Hot 50 Morgan Dollar Varieties* by Jeff Oxman, 2000.

The number of **desirability stars** is given for each variety from one to five with five being the most desirable. There are 9 **primary** overdate varieties (Not counting any sub-varieties.) with five stars and three with four stars. The rest have three stars or less because of the weaker evidence of the overdate, although two of the 1880 O VAM sub-varieties have five stars and two have four stars. Some new overdate die combinations of 1880 P VAM 53 and 1880 O VAM 63 were recently reported as well as five new clashed die letters sub-varieties.

The date and **person reporting** each variety is given in the extreme right column. The first Morgan dollar overdate of 1880 P VAM 6 was reported by George Mallis in his July 1964 booklet, *List of Die Varieties of Morgan Head Silver Dollars* followed by the 1880 CC VAM 4 reported by Harry Forman in August 1964 and 1880 CC VAMs 5 & 6 reported by Walter Breen in October 1964. The reporting of these strong 1880 CC overdates came soon after the Treasury Department stopped releasing silver dollars from it's vaults in March 1964. The public had a chance to examine uncirculated 1880 CC Morgan dollars from uncirculated bags released at the end of the stampede to clean out the Treasury Department vaults before most Carson City bags were set aside for later sales to the public by the General Services Administration (GSA) in the 1970's. These formerly rare 1880 CC dollars were discovered in mid and late 1964 to have prominent overdates. This was exciting front page news of the numismatic newspapers and precipitated an intensive search for other 1880 overdates. The rest of the currently known primary overdates, excluding the clashed dies sub-varieties, were reported in the late 1960's thru October 1978. Amazingly, no new primary 1880 overdates were reported since then, for over 25 years, until the 1880 O VAM 55 recently reported by Jeff Oxman in February 2005.

A short **description** of each overdate characteristics is given plus other primary die features such as doubled date digits or design features to allow quick identification of the die variety. Lastly, a general indication of the **premium price** currently commanded by the Top 100, Hot 50 and other varieties is pointed out.

1880 OVERDATES QUICK ATTRIBUTION SUMMARY

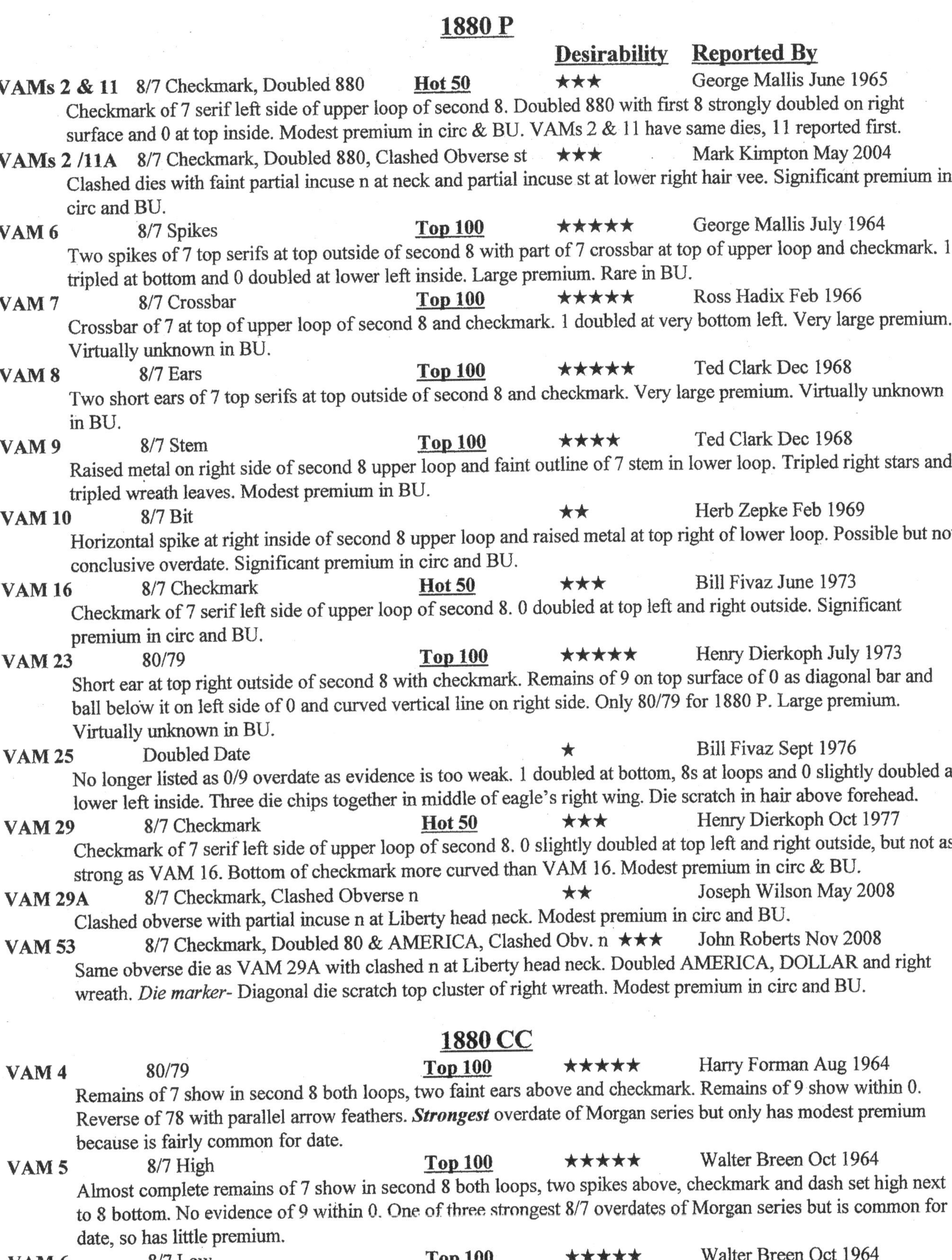

1880 P

Desirability **Reported By**

VAMs 2 & 11 8/7 Checkmark, Doubled 880 **Hot 50** ★★★ George Mallis June 1965
Checkmark of 7 serif left side of upper loop of second 8. Doubled 880 with first 8 strongly doubled on right surface and 0 at top inside. Modest premium in circ & BU. VAMs 2 & 11 have same dies, 11 reported first.

VAMs 2 /11A 8/7 Checkmark, Doubled 880, Clashed Obverse st ★★★ Mark Kimpton May 2004
Clashed dies with faint partial incuse n at neck and partial incuse st at lower right hair vee. Significant premium in circ and BU.

VAM 6 8/7 Spikes **Top 100** ★★★★★ George Mallis July 1964
Two spikes of 7 top serifs at top outside of second 8 with part of 7 crossbar at top of upper loop and checkmark. 1 tripled at bottom and 0 doubled at lower left inside. Large premium. Rare in BU.

VAM 7 8/7 Crossbar **Top 100** ★★★★★ Ross Hadix Feb 1966
Crossbar of 7 at top of upper loop of second 8 and checkmark. 1 doubled at very bottom left. Very large premium. Virtually unknown in BU.

VAM 8 8/7 Ears **Top 100** ★★★★★ Ted Clark Dec 1968
Two short ears of 7 top serifs at top outside of second 8 and checkmark. Very large premium. Virtually unknown in BU.

VAM 9 8/7 Stem **Top 100** ★★★★ Ted Clark Dec 1968
Raised metal on right side of second 8 upper loop and faint outline of 7 stem in lower loop. Tripled right stars and tripled wreath leaves. Modest premium in BU.

VAM 10 8/7 Bit ★★ Herb Zepke Feb 1969
Horizontal spike at right inside of second 8 upper loop and raised metal at top right of lower loop. Possible but not conclusive overdate. Significant premium in circ and BU.

VAM 16 8/7 Checkmark **Hot 50** ★★★ Bill Fivaz June 1973
Checkmark of 7 serif left side of upper loop of second 8. 0 doubled at top left and right outside. Significant premium in circ and BU.

VAM 23 80/79 **Top 100** ★★★★★ Henry Dierkoph July 1973
Short ear at top right outside of second 8 with checkmark. Remains of 9 on top surface of 0 as diagonal bar and ball below it on left side of 0 and curved vertical line on right side. Only 80/79 for 1880 P. Large premium. Virtually unknown in BU.

VAM 25 Doubled Date ★ Bill Fivaz Sept 1976
No longer listed as 0/9 overdate as evidence is too weak. 1 doubled at bottom, 8s at loops and 0 slightly doubled at lower left inside. Three die chips together in middle of eagle's right wing. Die scratch in hair above forehead.

VAM 29 8/7 Checkmark **Hot 50** ★★★ Henry Dierkoph Oct 1977
Checkmark of 7 serif left side of upper loop of second 8. 0 slightly doubled at top left and right outside, but not as strong as VAM 16. Bottom of checkmark more curved than VAM 16. Modest premium in circ & BU.

VAM 29A 8/7 Checkmark, Clashed Obverse n ★★ Joseph Wilson May 2008
Clashed obverse with partial incuse n at Liberty head neck. Modest premium in circ and BU.

VAM 53 8/7 Checkmark, Doubled 80 & AMERICA, Clashed Obv. n ★★★ John Roberts Nov 2008
Same obverse die as VAM 29A with clashed n at Liberty head neck. Doubled AMERICA, DOLLAR and right wreath. *Die marker*- Diagonal die scratch top cluster of right wreath. Modest premium in circ and BU.

1880 CC

VAM 4 80/79 **Top 100** ★★★★★ Harry Forman Aug 1964
Remains of 7 show in second 8 both loops, two faint ears above and checkmark. Remains of 9 show within 0. Reverse of 78 with parallel arrow feathers. ***Strongest*** overdate of Morgan series but only has modest premium because is fairly common for date.

VAM 5 8/7 High **Top 100** ★★★★★ Walter Breen Oct 1964
Almost complete remains of 7 show in second 8 both loops, two spikes above, checkmark and dash set high next to 8 bottom. No evidence of 9 within 0. One of three strongest 8/7 overdates of Morgan series but is common for date, so has little premium.

VAM 6 8/7 Low **Top 100** ★★★★★ Walter Breen Oct 1964
Almost complete remains of 7 show in second 8 both loops, two spikes above, checkmark and low dash below 8. No evidence of 9 with 0. One of three strongest 8/7 overdates of Morgan series but is common for date, so has little premium.

VAM 7 8/7 Dash ★★★ Ted Clark Oct 1970

Part of left ear at top left outside of second 8, two raised diagonal lines and die chip on right inside of lower loop and dash below. Reverse of 78 with parallel arrow feathers. Little premium.

VAM 7A 8/7 Dash, Clashed Obverse n ★★★ Phil Perdue May 2006

Clashed obverse with partial incuse n at Liberty head neck. Little premium.

VAM 8 8/7 Dash ★★ Ted Clark Oct 1970

Same obverse as VAM 7 but polished down with just dash below second 8. Small CC mint mark have dot in center of each C. Little premium.

VAM 9 8/7 Dash ★★ Ted Clark Oct 1970

Same obverse as VAM 7 but polished down with just dash below second 8. Large CC mint mark. Little premium.

1880 O

VAM 4 80/79 **Top 100** ★★★★★ Walter Breen Feb 1966

Partial horizontal bar in top loop of second 8, faint short ear at top right outside, checkmark. 0 has small raised metal at top right inside. Doubled 188. Micro I O mint mark. Significant premium in higher BU.

VAM 5 8/7 Ear **Top 100** ★★★★ Ted Clark Nov 1968

Partial horizontal bar inside top loop of second 8 with faint ear at top left outside, faint checkmark. No raised metal inside 0. Die scratch between eagle's left wing and neck. Medium tall oval II O mint mark. Significant premium in higher BU.

VAM 6 8/7 Spike **Top 100** ★★★★★ Ross Hadix Apr 1966

Long spike at top left outside of second 8 with small horizontal spike at right inside of upper loop, checkmark. Much scarcer than other varieties with same obverse. Micro I O mint mark. Significant premium in circ and BU.

VAM 6A 8/7 Spike, Clashed die n &st **Top 100** ★★★★ Ted Clark Nov 1968

Same obverse as VAM 6 but with clashed die with faint incuse n at neck and incuse st in lower right hair vee. Die gouge in left wreath. Micro I O mint mark. Modest premium in circ and BU.

VAM 6B/49 8/7 Spike, Hangnail Eagle **Top 100** ★★★★★ Ted Clark Nov 1968

Same obverse as VAM 6A with clashed n & st. Die gouge at bottom of 7th tail feather, so-called hangnail eagle. UNITED letters doubled towards rim that made this VAM 49. Micro I O mint mark. Large premium in circ & BU.

VAM 6C 8/7 Spike, Clashed Die Obv In, We, ust, Rev M ★★★★★ Mark Kimpton May 2003

Same obverse as VAM 6 but strongly clashed dies with partial incuse In next to Liberty head neck and We & ust of Trust from reverse in lower hair edge. Raised designer's initial M from obverse above d in God. Micro I O mint mark. Significant premium in circ and BU.

VAM 6D 8/7 Spike, Clashed Obverse st ★★★★ Laurence Galbraith Dec 2007

Same clashed obverse die n & st as VAMs 6A & 6B/49. Reverse die not clashed without die gouge in left wreath or hangnail die gouge, early die state of VAM 6C reverse. Modest prium in circ and BU.

VAM 16 8/7 Checkmark **Hot 50** ★★★ Leroy Van Allen July 1976

Checkmark of 7 serif left side of upper loop of second 8 and short vertical bar on surface at right side of loops junction. Micro I O mint mark. Modest premium in circ and BU.

VAM 17 8/7 Checkmark **Hot 50** ★★★ Leroy Van Allen Dec 1976

Same obverse as VAM 16. Medium II O oval mint mark at normal height. Significant premium in circ and BU.

VAM 21 8/7 Checkmark **Hot 50** ★★★ Henry Dierkoph Nov 1977

Checkmark of 7 serif left side of upper loop of second 8 and vertical line at upper right of lower loop. Slightly doubled 880 & eye front, so-called alligator eye. Micro I O mint mark. Modest premium in circ and BU.

VAM 25 8/7 Spike ★★★★ Jim Baxter Oct 1978

Same obverse as VAM 6. Micro I O mint mark set high and to right. Modest premium in circ and BU.

VAM 49 8/7 Spike, Hangnail Eagle

See VAM 6B. VAM 49 is later die designation with doubled reverse added that was reported by Randy Campbell in April 1999.

VAM 55 8/7 Checkmark ★★★ Jeff Oxman Feb 2005

Checkmark of 7 serif left side of upper loop of second 8. Doubled reverse legend letters and some wreath leaves. Micro O mint mark centered. Significant premium in circ and BU.

VAM 63 8/7 Checkmark, Medium O mint mark ★★ Clayton Christiansen Mar 2006

Same 8/7 checkmark as VAMs 16 & 17. Medium II O oval mint mark set high. Significant premium in circ & BU.

1880 S

VAM 8 80/79 Ear **Top 100** ★★★ Ted Clark Dec 1968

Raised metal in most of second 8 upper loop with horizontal line just below metal. Faint spike top left outside of second 8 and small raised area top right inside of 0. Medium S mint mark. Modest premium in circ and BU.

VAM 9 80/79 Ear **Top 100** ★★★ Ted Clark Mar 1969

Same obverse die as VAM 8 but reverse has large S mint mark that is doubled to left of top serif. Modest premium in circ and BU.

VAM 10 8/7 Crossbar **Top 100** ★★★ Ted Clark Feb 1969

Horizontal line bottom inside upper loop of second 8. Early strikes have thin bars and dots in middle of upper loop and faint dots at top left and right outside. Doubled 188 and reverse legend letters and wreath leaves. Modest premium in circ and BU.

VAM 11 0/9 **Hot 50** ★★★ James Cornish Apr 1967

Wide vertical area intersecting top inside of 0 with notch at top left with heavy polishing lines. Similar to top right inside of 1880 CC VAM 4 80/79. Controversial overdate as remains aren't clearly a partial 9. Doubled 1-8 and S/S. Modest premium for circ and BU.

VAM 12 8/7 Spikes ★★★ Gordon Harnack Oct 1972

Checkmark of 7 serif left side of upper loop of second 8, spike ear at top left of 8 loop and small raised metal area at top inside of 0. Doubled 188. Only a little premium for circ and BU.

MORGAN DOLLAR 1880 OVERDATES

The VAM book lists many overdate varieties for the 1880 and the two obvious and non-controversial 1887/6. Quite a few of the overdates for the various 1880 P, CC, O and S mints are also obvious. But a number are very subtle with weak evidence and thus ***marginal*** in acceptance and value. In his 1998 book *Morgan Dollar Overdates, Misplaced Dates and Clashed E Reverses,* Kevin Flynn refuted ten of the 1880 overdates and listed three others as only possible overdates. Their evidence or lack thereof for these refuted overdates will be examined in later paragraphs.

Ted Clark had examined the case for most of the Morgan overdates in a lengthy series of ***in-depth*** *Coin World Collectors' Clearinghouse* articles in the November/December 1970 and again in January– April 1973 issues. His analyses served the basis for the overdate listings in the 1976 second edition VAM book and later 1992 third edition VAM book. As Ted Clark's articles are now over 35 years old, it is timely to briefly review the 1880 Morgan overdate evidence on those listed in the current 1998 fourth edition VAM book. Only one new overdate, two new overdate die combinations and five new sub-varieties have been reported since publishing of the 1992 third edition VAM book.

Overdate Simulations

In order to show how the underlying digit remains might show inside, outside and on top of the punched in overlying digit, superimposed photos are provided in the accompanying page. The digits of Morgan dollar dates were photographed for the 7 and 9 from 1879 coins and 8 and 0 digits from 1880 coins. The digit photographs were superimposed in various relative positions to show high and low overdates. Note the "ears" of the 7 that appear above the 8 top loop and the 7 crossbar that can just appear in part of the upper loop opening or almost the entire loop opening of the 8. A form of a checkmark is on the surface of the left side of the upper loop from the 7 lower serif. There can also be the bottom of the 7 shaft showing as a dash below the lower loop if the 8 is punched with 7 in a lower position.

If the 0 digit is punched centered over the 9 digit, then a fairly good match occurs for the left and right sides and the top and bottom. Only the thin lower part of the 9 upper loop crosses the center of the 0 digit. This can explain why there are few examples of much of the remains of the 9 that can be seen in the 1880 over 1879 overdates. If the 9 and 0 are out of alignment however, then some of the right or left side of the 9 loops a could show within the 0 center.

The plastic three-dimensional metal flow that occurs when the 80 digits are punched over 79 digits was simulated using the digits carved into the end of wooden blocks from photo overlays of the coin digit photos. These wooden digits were pressed into modeling clay to simulate one digit being forced over another. Wax casts were then made of the clay molds to show how the raised digits of a coin might appear. Again the ears of the 7 appear above the 8 upper loop with the 7 crossbar within the upper loop of the 8. If the impression of the 8 was at the same depth as the 7, there shows quite a bit of detail of the 7 on top of the 8. When the 8 was impressed deeper than the 7, there were much weaker remains on the 8 surface as could be expected. The 0 over the 9 wax cast with the 0 digit shifted to the right shows the remains of the right side of the 9 within the 0. Since the 8 digit is wider than the 7 digit, it was likely that the 0 had to be punched a little to the right of the 9 in order to maintain the same relative spacing between digits.

1880 P Overdates

The 1880 P overdate varieties are listed as 8/7, 0/9 or 80/79 for VAMs 2, 6, 7, 8, 9, 10, 11, 16, 23, 25, 29 & 53. VAM 2 was reported by Bill Fivaz in February 1973, VAM 6 by George Mallis in July 1964, VAM 7 by Ross Haddix in February 1966, VAM 8 by Ted Clark in December 1970, VAM 9 by Ted Clark in December 1968, VAM 10 by Herb Zepke in February 1969, VAM 11 by George Mallis in June 1965, VAM 16 by Bill Fivaz in June 1973, VAM 23 by Henry Dierkoph in July 1976, VAM 25 by Bill Fivaz in September 1976, VAM 29 by Henry Dierkoph in October 1977 and VAM 53

1879 O VAM 4
7 Example

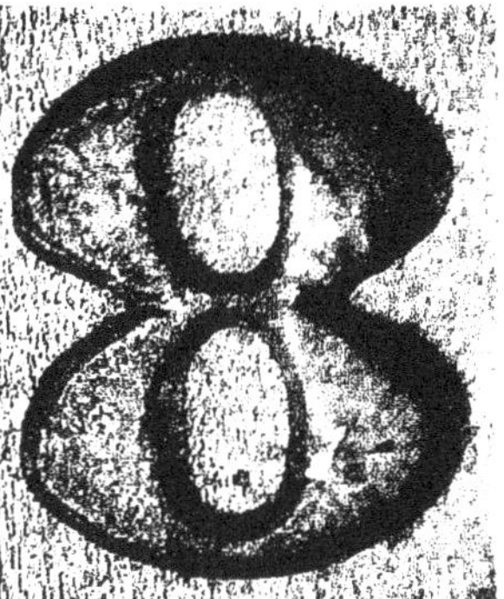
1880 O VAM 30
8 Example

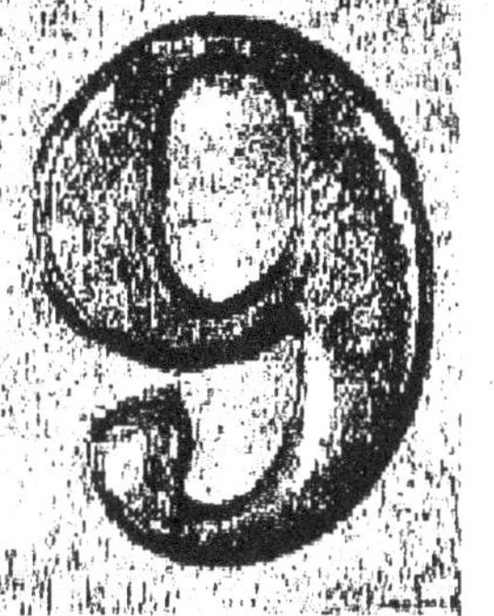
1879 P VAM 49
9 Example

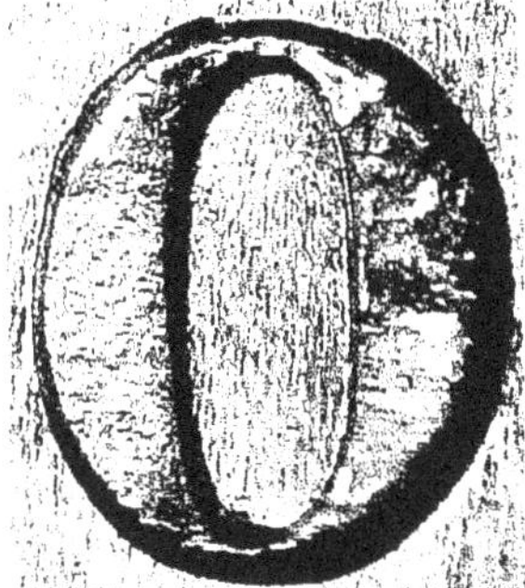
1880 S VAM 21
0 Example

8/7 High 7
Photo Superposition

8/7 Low 7
Photo Superposition

0/9 Centered 9
Photo Superposition

0/9 Left 9
Photo Superposition

7 & 8 Wooden Date Digits

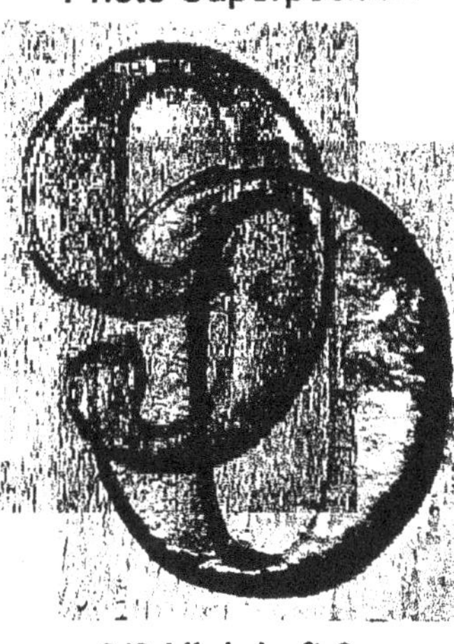
0/9 High Left 9
Photo Superposition

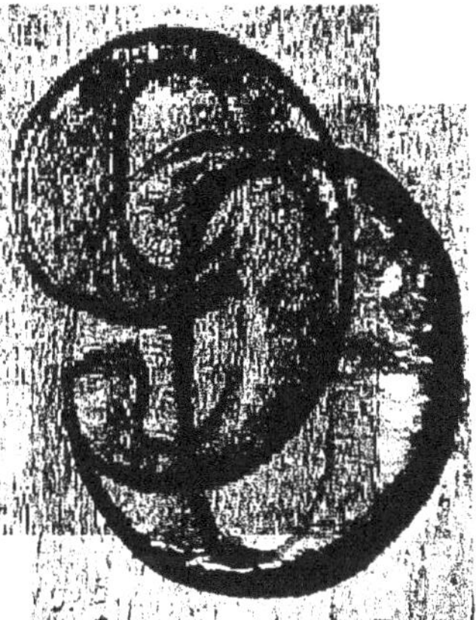
0/9 High 9
Photo Superposition

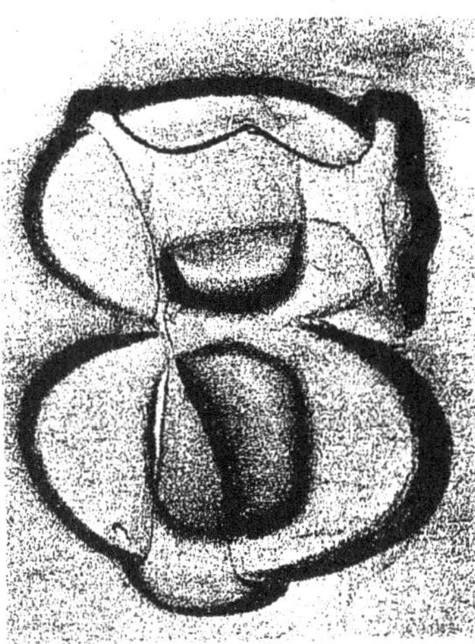
8/7 Clay Mold
7 & 8 Same Depth

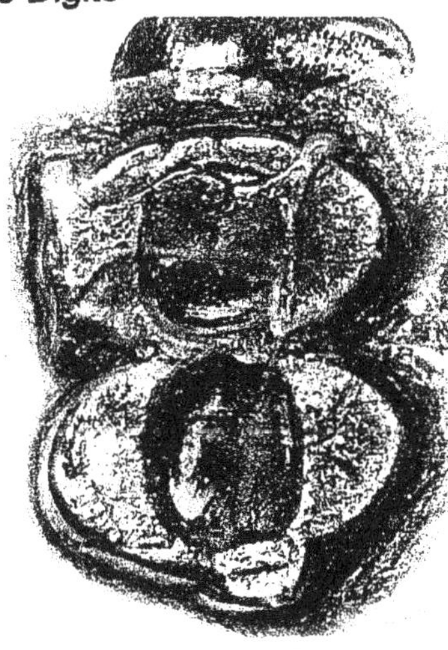
8/7 Wax Cast
7 & 8 Same Depth

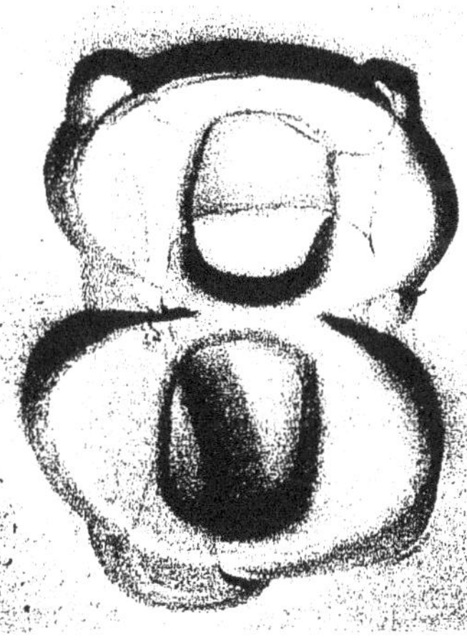
8/7 Clay Mold
8 Deeper Than 7

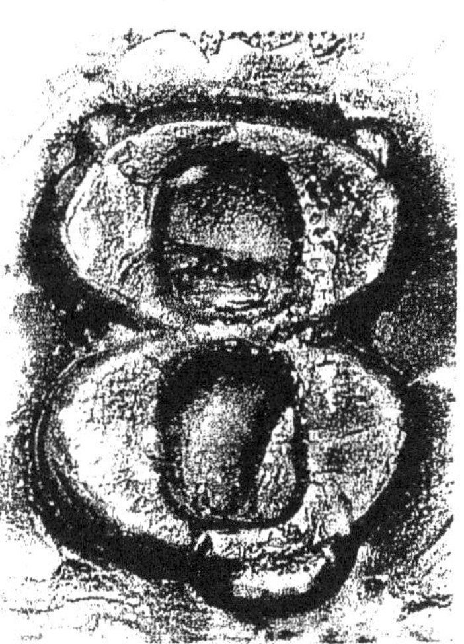
8/7 Wax Cast
8 Deeper Than 7

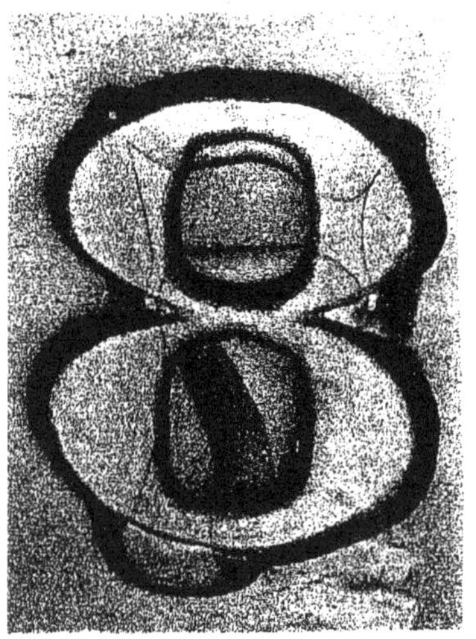

8/7 Clay Mold 7 Set Low

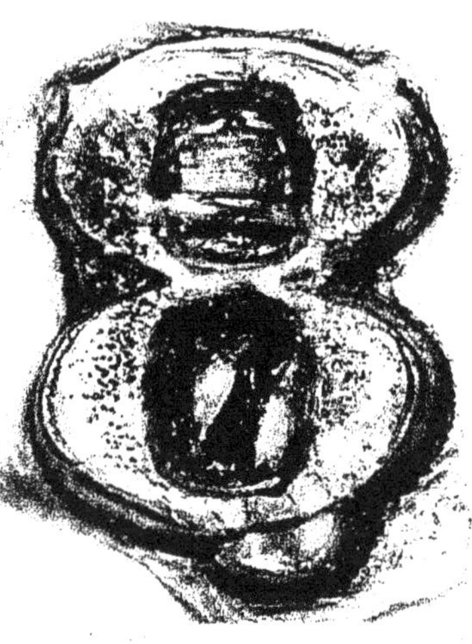

8/7 Wax Cast 7 Set Low

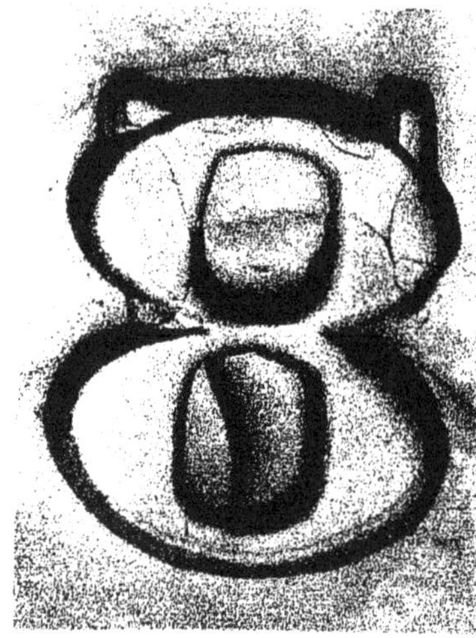

8/7 Clay Mold 7 Set High

8/7 Wax Cast 7 Set High

9 Wooden Block

0 (zero) Wooden Block

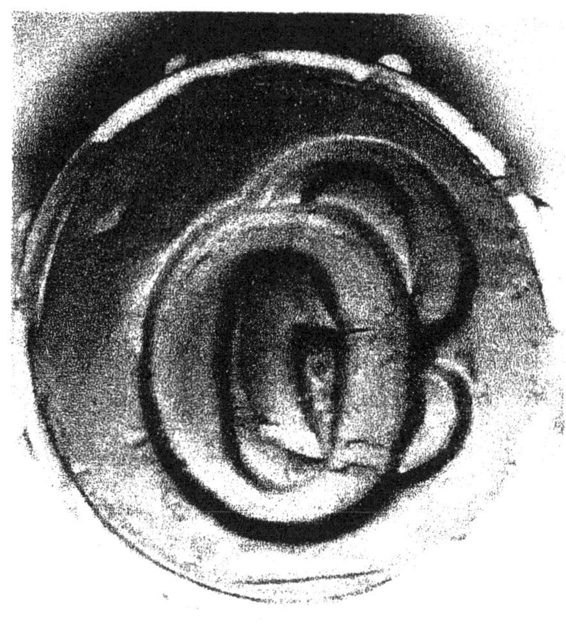

0/9 Clay Mold Impressions

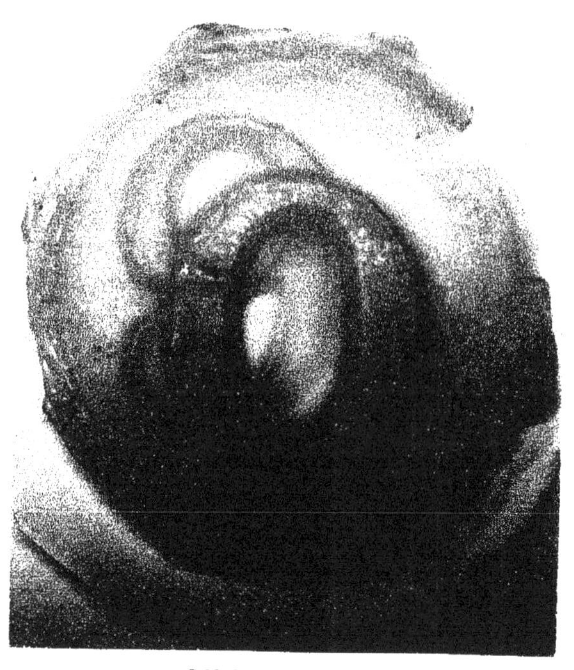

0/9 Wax Casting

by John Roberts in November 2008. Sub-varieties, VAM 2/11A, with clashed st letters on obverse was reported by Mark Kimpton in May 2004 and VAM 29A with clashed n letter on obverse was reported by Joseph Wilson in May 2008.

Actually VAMs 2 and 11 are the ***same*** 8/7 checkmark dies and file photos of each variety show the whole date matching up. The 1976 VAM book had been marked that they were the same variety but somehow it didn't get into the 1992 VAM book. VAM 2 should be eliminated since VAM 11 has the more correct description of the doubled 880 and was reported earlier in 1965 than VAM 2 in 1973. That leaves 10 listed 1880 P different overdates and one with a different reverse die, VAM 53. VAMs 6, 7 & 8 are obvious non-controversial 8/7 and VAM 23 has strong non-controversial evidence of 7 and 9 on top of 8 and 0. The remaining six are weaker or controversial overdates.

VAM 6 8/7 Spikes shown in Figures 1 and 2 has two obvious ear spikes above the upper loop of the second 8 with a horizontal crossbar in the upper loop and a checkmark on the left side of the upper loop. It also has a doubled date with the 1 and first 8 doubled at bottom outside, second 8 at lower left outside of the upper loop and at the left inside.

VAM 7 8/7 Crossbar of Figure 3 shows a horizontal crossbar at the top of the upper loop of the second 8 and a checkmark on the left side of the upper loop. 1 is doubled at very bottom.

VAM 8 8/7 Ears of Figure 4 has two short ears above the upper loop of the second 8 and a checkmark on the left side of the upper loop. Only a small raised metal is at right inside of the upper loop.

The ***unusual*** 80/79 overdate of **VAM 23** is shown in Figures 16 and 17 with a checkmark on the left side of the second 8 upper loop and a short ear at top right outside. Remains of the 9 are on the surface of the 0 as a diagonal bar and ball below it on the left side and curved line on the right side. The 1 and first 8 are doubled at the bottom. This variety is an obvious strong overdate on the surfaces of the 80.

VAMs 6, 7, 8, & 23 are all Top 100 varieties and command large premiums.

VAM 2/11 8/7 Checkmark shown in Figures 11 and 12 has an obvious checkmark on the surface of the left side of the second 8 upper loop which is the lower left serif of the 7 crossbar. This shows up on VAMs 6, 7 and 8 in conjunction with raised metal remains of 7 crossbar in the 8 upper loop and ears or spikes above the 8 top loop which are the 7 upper serifs. VAM 2/11 also shows a doubled 880 with the first 8 strongly doubled on the right top surface and 0 at top inside. A Hot 50 variety that has a modest premium. The sub-variety **VAM 2/11A** has clashed dies with a faint tick of incuse n of In from reverse next to the neck shown in Figure 13 and a faint partial incuse st of Trust shown in Figure 14 from the reverse showing in the right hair vee of the lower hair edge.

VAMs 16 and 29 8/7 Checkmark shown in Figures 15 and 23 show clear checkmarks from the 7 lower serif on the left surface of the top loop of the second 8 which is very strong evidence of an overdate. But they don't command the large price premiums of the more obvious VAMs 6, 7 and 8 overdates. Flynn had refuted VAM 16 but photos in his book don't match up with those of the VAM book. So his photos must be of a different variety. Flynn didn't mention VAM 29. Both VAMs 16 and 29 show doubling at the top right and left of the 0 but VAM 29 isn't as strong as VAM 16. VAM 29 shows a small die chip in the upper inside of the left 8 lower loop as shown in Figure 22. VAM 29 also shows a short die gouge in Go of God as shown in Figure 24. **VAM 29A** has a partial clashed incuse n at the Liberty head neck as shown in Figure 25. VAMs 16 and 29 are both Hot 50 varieties with modest premiums. **VAM 53** has the same 8/7 checkmark as VAM 29 but a different reverse die with slightly doubled AMERICA and right wreath and fine die scratch at top of right wreath as shown in Figures 26 & 27.

VAM 25 0/9 is a questionable 0/9 which Flynn didn't mention. It has some raised metal and a dot showing on the left side of the 0 surface that is hard to relate to a 9, and nothing on the second 8 as shown in Figure 19. It has slight doubling at the bottom of the 1, doubled 8s loops and lower left inside of the 0 as shown in Figure 18. VAM 25 is eliminated as an 0/9 overdate and just listed as a double date. VAM 25 has a thin polishing line in the hair above the forehead as shown in Figure 20 and three

Figure 1 1880 P VAM 6 8/7 Spikes, Doubled Date

Figure 2 1880 P VAM 6 8/7 Spikes, Doubled Date

Figure 3 1880 P VAM 7 8/7 Crossbar

Figure 4 1880 P VAM 8 8/7 Ears

Figure 5 1880 P VAM 9 8/7 Stem

Figure 6 1880 P VAM 9 8/7 Stem, Doubled Date

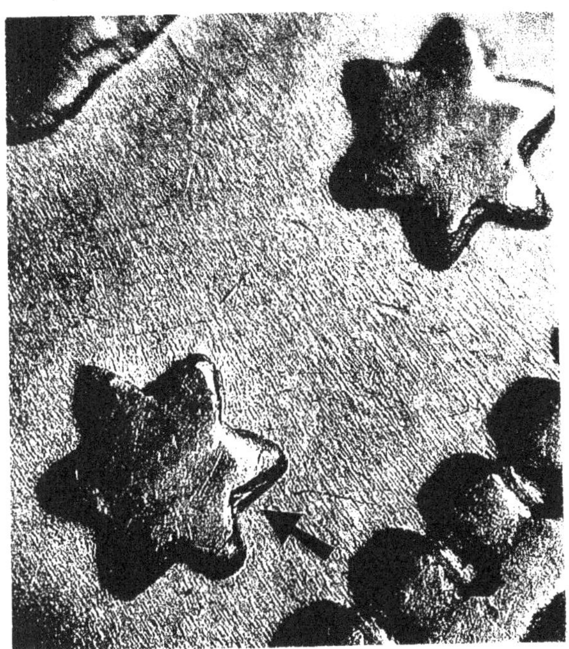

Figure 7 1880 P VAM 9 8/7 Stem, Tripled Rt. Stars

Figure 8 1880 P VAM 9 8/7 Stem, Tripled Wreath Leaves

Figure 9 1880 P VAM 10 8/7 Bit

Figure 10 1880 P VAM 10 Die Scratches

Figure 11 1880 P VAM 2/11 Doubled 8

Figure 12 VAM 2/11 Doubled 80, Checkmark

Figure 13 1880 P VAM 2/11A Clashed n

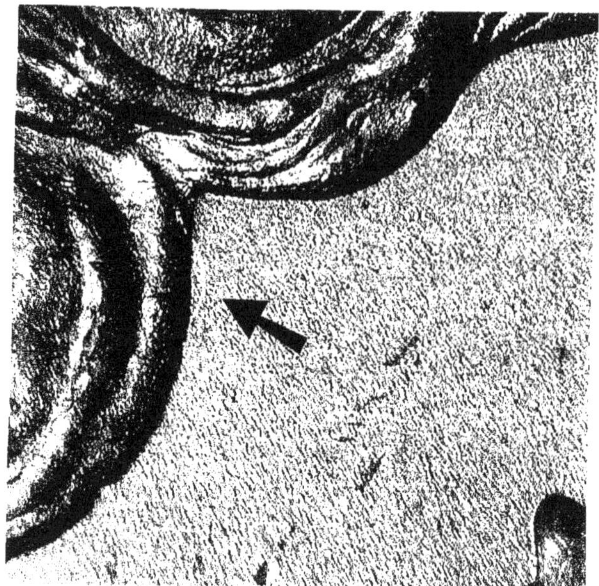

Figure 14 1880 P VAM 11A Clashed st

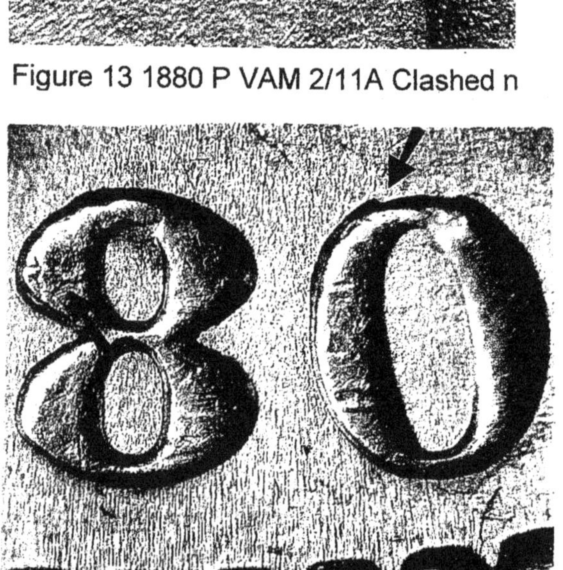

Figure 15 1880 P VAM 16 8/7 Checkmark, Doubled 80

Figure 16 1880 P VAM 23 Doubled 18

Figure 17 1880 P VAM 23 80/79

Figure 18 1880 P VAM 25 Doubled 18

Figure 19 1880 P VAM 25 Doubled 80

Figure 20 1880 P VAM 25 Die Scratch Forehead & Hair

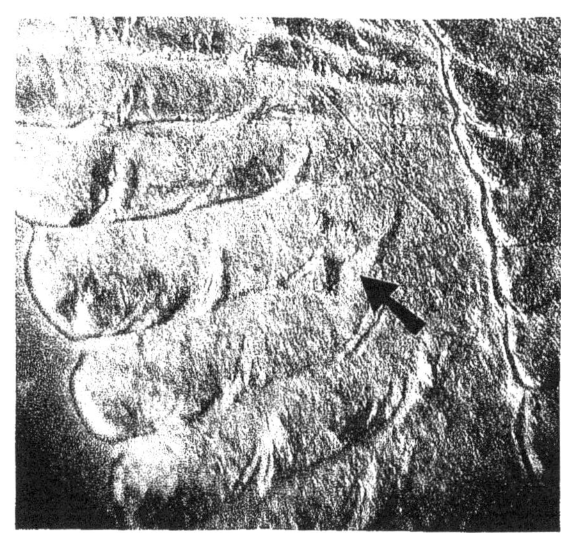

Figure 21 1880 P VAM 25 Die Chips Wing

Figure 22 1880 P VAM 29 Die Chip 8 Loop

Figure 23 1880 P VAM 29 8/7 Checkmark, Doubled 0

Figure 24 1880 P VAM 29 Die Gouge Go

Figure 25 1880 P VAM 29A Clashed n

Figure 26 1880 P VAM 53 Die Scratch Rt. Wreath Top

Figure 27 1880 P VAM 53 Doubled AMERICA, Wreath

small die chips together in the middle of the eagle's right wing as shown in Figure 21.

That leaves VAMs 9 and 10 which Flynn had labeled as possible and refuted overdates respectively.

VAM 9 8/7 Stem shown in Figures 5, 6, 7 & 8 has raised metal in the right inside of the upper loop of the second 8 at the same positions as the 1880 CC VAMs 4 and 5 non-controversial overdates. In the words of Ted Clark in his article on Morgan dollar overdates that discussed the 1880 P VAM 9 in the *Collectors' Clearinghouse, Coin World* December 9, 1970 issue:

"One visible remnant of the 7 remaining is a small piece of extra metal from the crossbar appearing about 3 o'clock near the inside rim of the top loop of the 8. It is in the same position as on the start of the crossbar on the 1880/7 CC, variety 1, high 7 (now listed as VAM 5)."

"Inside the bottom loop of the 8 are two pieces of the stem, one is easily seen and is the top left portion of the stem. It starts out at about 1 o'clock (as a line) from the inside rim at a 45 degree angle, and continues for a short distance downward. Also, it starts out exactly at the same point with the same angle as the stem on variety 1, 1880/7 CC, but is of more substance than on most CC stems."

"Below and between it and the 8's inside rim is another piece of extra metal. On one specimen, more of the stem's almost complete faint outline can be seen..."

Early die states also show almost a complete outline of the 7 stem in the lower loop and also displays a faint checkmark on the left side of the second 8 upper loop. It also has tripled right stars shown in Figure 7 and tripled wreath leaves shown in Figure 8. With some key overdate evidence within the 8 loops, VAM 9 is a Top 100 variety and commands a modest premium, particularly in high grade BU.

VAM 10 8/7 Bit shown in Figure 9 is described in the VAM book as a possible 8/7 but evidence is not conclusive. It has two horizontal spikes or a large spike on the right inside of the second 8 upper loop depending on the die state. These spikes are in the same position as the 7 crossbar in the upper loop of the second 8 of 1880 CC VAMs 4, 5 and 6. It also shows some faint raised metal at the right inside edge of the second 8 lower loop from 12 to 4 o'clock. There is no checkmark or ears on the second 8. It could be a re-punched 8 although the doubling outline is usually sharper and more defined for die doubling. The trouble is that the raised metal is in the same position as that shown by the more stronger 1880 overdates which makes it a suspected overdate but the evidence is not conclusive. The eagle's right wing has two long die scratches for die markers as shown in Figure 10.

So the 1880 P ends up with ***four*** strong overdates of VAMs 6, 7, 8 and 23; ***one*** moderate overdate of VAM 9; ***three*** overdates with just the checkmarks showing of VAMs 2/11, 16 and 29 with ***one*** shared VAM 29 obverse with VAM 53; ***two*** clashed die sub-variety of VAMs 2/11A & 29A; and the ***one*** possible but not conclusive VAM 10. The questionable VAM 25 is eliminated as an 0/9 overdate and is listed as only a doubled date. Thus there are a total of **12** listed overdate die varieties for the 1880 P.

1880 CC Overdates

There are 1880 CC overdate varieties listed as 80/79 and 8/7 as follows: VAMs 4, 5, 6, 7, 8, 9 and 10. VAM 4 was reported by Harry Forman in August 1964, VAMs 5 & 6 by Walter Breen in October 1964, VAMs 7, 8 and 9 by Ted Clark in October 1970, VAM 7A by Phil Perdue in May 2006 and VAM 10 by Hoyt Warren in March 1973.

VAM 4 80/79 has the most ***dramatic*** and ***clear*** evidence of 80/79 in the Morgan dollar series with remains of the 7 and 9 bold and almost complete inside the 8 and 0 as shown in Figure 28. There are faint ears above the 8 and a checkmark from the 7 lower serif on the surface of the left side of the 8 upper loop. It has the reverse of 78 with parallel arrow feathers.

VAM 5 8/7 High shows the crossbar in the upper loop and stem of the 7 within the 8 with two ears above the top loop and a thin dash below the bottom loop. A checkmark from the 7 lower serif shows on the left side of the upper loop as shown in Figure 30. The first 8 is doubled at the top inside of the lower loops shown in Figure 29. No remains of the 9 show inside or on top of the 0.

VAM 6 8/7 Low shows similar 7 remains as VAM 5 but with the 7 crossbar and dash set

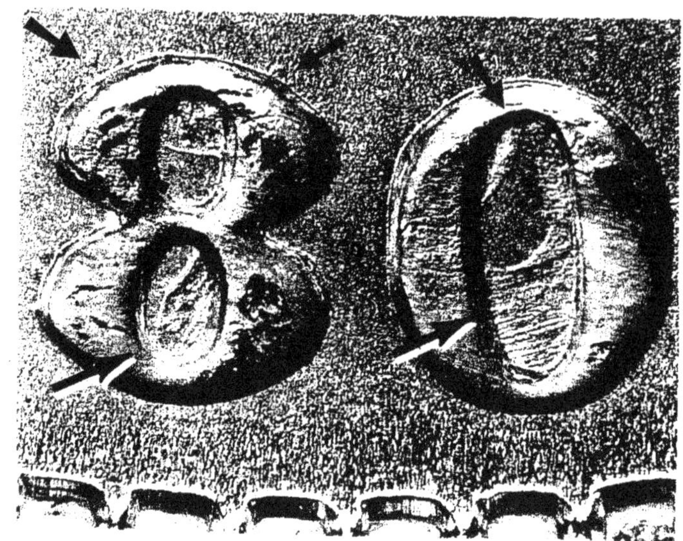

Figure 28 1880 CC VAM 4 80/79

Figure 29 1880 CC VAM 5 Doubled 8

Figure 30 1880 CC VAM 5 8/7 High

Figure 31 1880 CC VAM 6 8/7 Low

Figure 32 1880 CC VAM 6/8 CC Dots

lower. A small raised metal with polishing lines shows at the bottom inside within the 0 as pictured in Figure 31. The small CC mint mark has dots within them shown in Figure 32 which is shared with VAM 8.

Although VAMs 4, 5 & 6 are the strongest appearing overdates of the Morgan dollars, the GSA sold 115,000 uncirculated 1880 CC in the 1970's. These strong overdates of VAMs 4, 5 & 6 were fairly common in that hoard making them readily available varieties of the 1880 CC date. Therefore, they have little premium value even though they are all Top 100 listed varieties since even the non-overdate 1880 CC are priced fairly high.

VAMs 7, 8 and 9 8/7 Dash share the same obverse dies with VAMs 8 and 9 being later polished down die states paired with different reverses as shown in Figures 33 & 35. The early die state VAM 7 shows part of the top left serif or ear at top left outside of the second 8, two raised diagonal lines and die chips on the right side and top inside in the lower loop of the 8 and a raised horizontal dash just below the bottom of the second 8. The right ear at the top outside and 7 crossbar do not show on the 8. VAM 7 has the earlier reverse of 78 with parallel arrow feathers. The later die states of VAMs 8 and 9 only show the dash under the 8. VAM 8 has the reverse of 79 with slanted arrow feathers and small CC mint mark. VAM 9 has the reverse of 79 with large CC mint marks. Since VAM 7 shows some weak evidence of the 7 remains of the top left ear, raised lines and die chips in the lower loop and dash below the 8, VAMs 7, 8 and 9 are likely overdates. Flynn had refuted VAMs 7, 8 and 9 as not being overdates, but that conclusion was based only on the photos of the later polished down dies of VAMs 8 and 9. The sub-variety **VAM 7A** has clashed dies with a faint incuse n of In from reverse next to the Liberty head neck as shown in Figure 34.

VAM 10 Dash & Doubled 8 shown in Figure 36 only shows a faint dash under the second 8 which Flynn refuted as an overdate. The dash by itself is not enough evidence of a 7 under the 8 as the listed 1880 CC VAM 3 also has a dash and is not considered an overdate. In addition, there are many other dates that just show a short dash under the second 8 which is considered a date logotype ***positioning*** mark. So as Flynn suggests, VAM 10 should not be considered an overdate. Originally it was mistakenly thought that VAM 10 was a polished down VAM 5, but that was disproved and the label of 8/7 probably just got carried over in error!

That leaves the 1880 CC with ***three*** of the strongest 80/79 and 8/7 overdates of the entire Morgan dollar series of VAMs 4, 5 and 6; plus ***three*** weak overdates of VAMs 7, 8 and 9 that have the same obverse die but in various die states but paired with different reverse dies; and a clashed die sub-variety of VAM 7A. Thus, there are a total of **seven** listed overdate die varieties for the 1880 CC.

1880 O Overdates

The 1880 O overdate varieties are listed as 80/79 and 8/7 as follows: VAMs 4, 5, 6, 6A & B (later became 49), 6C, 16, 17, 21, 25, 49 and 55. VAM 4 was reported by Walter Breen in February 1966, VAM 5 by Ted Clark in November 1968, VAM 6 by Ross Haddix in April 1966, VAMs 6A & 6B by Ted Clark in November 1968, VAM 6C by Mark Kimpton in May 2003, VAM 6D by Laurence Galbraith in December 2007, VAM 16 by Leroy Van Allen in July 1976, VAM 17 by Leroy Van Allen in December 1976, VAM 21 by Henry Dierkoph in November 1977, VAM 25 by Jim Baxter in October 1978, VAM 49 (revised 6B) by Randy Campbell in April 1999, VAM 55 by Jeff Oxman in February 2005 and VAM 63 by Clayton Christiansen in March 2006.

VAM 4 80/79 overdate shown in Figure 38 is the strongest non-controversial 1880 O overdate with a partial horizontal bar of raised metal in the upper loop, faint ear above the second 8 and a checkmark from the 7 lower serif on the top loop left side. The 0 has a small raised metal area at top right inside. It has a doubled 188 as shown in Figure 37 with small micro O mint mark. There is a significant premium for the higher grade BU for this Top 100 variety.

VAM 5 8/7 Ear overdate shown in Figure 39 is also non-controversial and has a partial horizontal bar of raised metal in the upper loop and a faint ear at top left of second 8 with a faint checkmark. It has a tall oval O mint mark. Also a Top 100 variety, it has a significant premium for the

Figure 33 1880 CC VAM 7 8/7 Dash

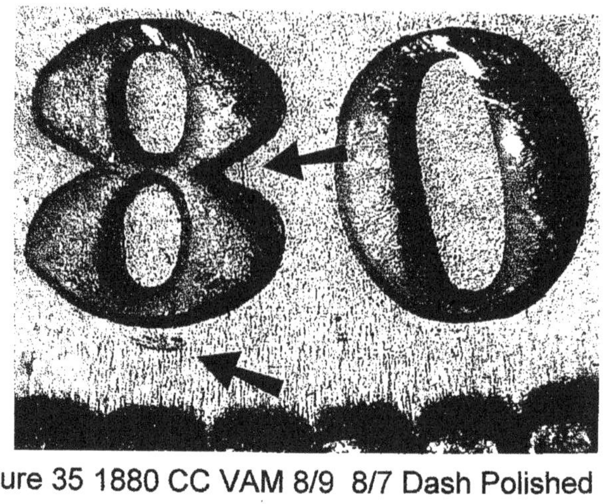

Figure 35 1880 CC VAM 8/9 8/7 Dash Polished

Figure 34 1880 CC VAM 7A Clashed n

Figure 36
1880 CC VAM 10
Doubled 88, Dash

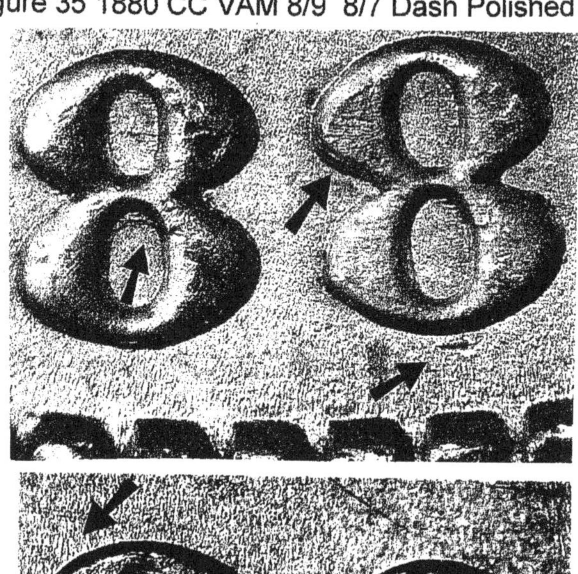

Figure 39 1880 O VAM 5 8/7 Ear

Figure 37 1880 O VAM 4 Doubled 188

Figure 38 1880 O VAM 4 80/79

higher grade BU.

VAM 6 8/7 Spike pictured in Figure 40 and sub-varieties 6A, 6B/49, 6C and 6D all show a long spike at top left outside, a small horizontal spike at the right inside of the upper loop and a clear checkmark from the 7 lower serif on the surface of the left side of the upper loop of the second 8. The reverse has a small micro O mint mark that is centered. This is an obvious non-controversial overdate and has a significant premium because of it's rarity and Top 100 variety.

VAM 6A has the same obverse die as VAM 6 but the reverse shows a die gouge in the top of the left wreath as shown in Figure 41. Although a Top 100 variety it has a modest premium because of its availability.

VAM 6B also has the same obverse as VAM 6 but with a die gouge at the bottom of the 7th tail feather, the so-called ***hangnail eagle*** as shown in Figure 42. It was later discovered to have slight doubling of UNITED letters on the reverse towards the rim and was made a separate variety, VAM 49, but the designations of 6B, 49 or 6B/49 all can be used. A Top 100 variety, it has a large premium.

VAM 6C has the same obverse as VAM 6 but shows severe die clashing with numerous die clash letters of incuse In next to Liberty head neck shown in Figure 43, incuse We and ust showing in the lower hair edge on the obverse and the raised letter M from the designer's initial M on the obverse showing above d in God on reverse. It has a significant premium.

VAM 6D has the same clashed obverse die as VAMs 6A & 6B/49. The reverse die is an early die state of VAM 6C <u>without</u> die clashes, hangnail die gouge or wreath die gouge. There is a die scratch in the left wreath first lower leaf cluster as shown in Figure 44 and a faint die crack between od and in God as shown in Figure 45. It has a modest premium.

VAM 25 8/7 Spike also has the same VAM 6 obverse but a different reverse die with a small micro O mint mark set high and to the right as shown in Fig 48. It only has a modest premium.

VAMs 16, 17 and 63 8/7 Checkmark have the same obverse pictured in Figure 46 which shows an obvious checkmark from the 7 lower serif on the left surface of the top loop of second 8 with a short vertical bar on the surface at right side of junction of 8 loops extending down into the side of top of lower loop opening from the 7 stem. This line is also obvious in the VAM book photos for 1880 P VAMs 9 and 23, 1880 CC VAM 5 and 1880 O VAM 4. Flynn called VAMs 16 and 17 possible but doubtful 8/7 because of the checkmark contour didn't match that of the bottom serif of 7 crossbar. However, the shape of the checkmarks on obvious overdates such as 1880 CC VAMs 4, 5 and 6 ***varies greatly*** probably due to the way the metal flowed in the 7 and 8 die cavities when the 8 was punched over the 7. The checkmark ***keys*** are the sharp raised lower ***point*** and somewhat ***straight*** vertical left side which is very unlikely for just die chips and rough die cavity surface. VAM 16 has a small micro I O mint mark and is a Hot 50 variety with a modest premium. VAM 17 has a medium oval II O mint mark at normal height, and is also a Hot 50 variety with a significant premium. VAM 63 also has a medium oval O mint mark but set high as shown in Figure 51, with a significant premium.

VAM 21 8/7 Checkmark shown in Figure 47 shows a weak checkmark from the 7 lower serif on the second 8 and a vertical line on the side of the lower loop opening at the upper right similar to VAMs 16 and 17. The VAM book photo of VAM 21 is not very clear in showing the checkmark, probably because of a lower grade coin used for the photo. Although not addressed by Flynn, there is convincing evidence that VAM 21 is a weak overdate. It has a slightly doubled eye front, a so-called alligator eye, to differentiate it from VAM 16 as they both have the small micro O mint mark. A Hot 50 variety with a modest premium.

VAM 55 8/7 Checkmark was the first ***new overdate*** to be reported in ***almost 30 years***!! It shows a new 8/7 checkmark from the 7 lower serif pictured in Figure 49 on the left side of the upper loop of the second 8 that is different than VAMs 16/17 and 21. There is no other evidence of an overdate, so it is a weak overdate. As shown in Figure 50, the reverse has some doubled legend letters and wreath leaves to differentiate it from VAMs 16/17/63 and 21. VAM 55 also has a small micro I O mint mark that is centered.

Thus, the 1880 O has ***two*** strong 80/79 and 8/7 of VAMs 4 and 5; ***one*** strong spike overdate of

Figure 40 1880 O VAM 6 8/7 Spike

Figure 41 1880 O VAM 6A Die Gouge Left Wreath

Figure 42 1880 O VAM 6B/49 Hangnail Die Gouge

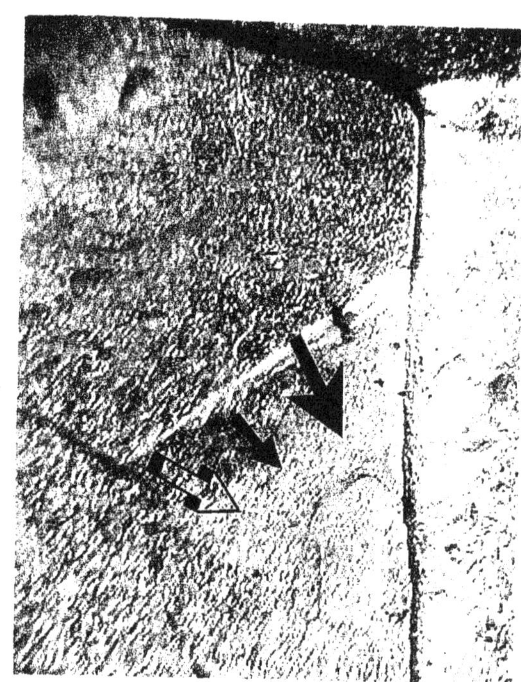

Figure 43 1880 O VAM 6C Clashed Die In

Figure 44 1880 O VAM 6D Die Scratch Leaf

Figure 45 VAM 6D Die Crack o-d

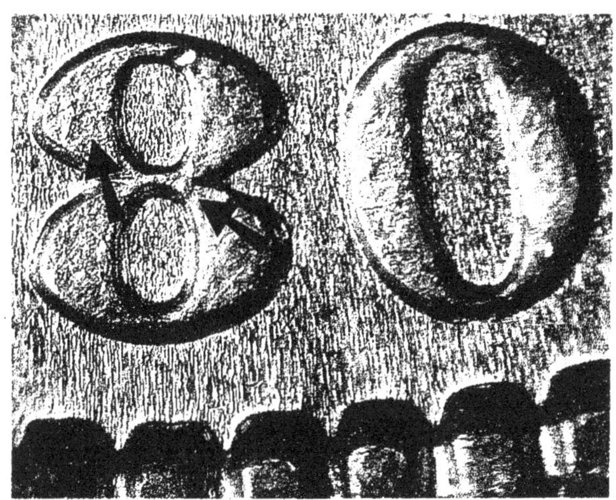

Figure 46 1880 O VAM 16 8/7 Checkmark, Shaft Bit

Figure 47 1880 O VAM 21 8/7 Checkmark, Shaft Bit

Figure 48 1880 O VAM 25 Micro O Set High & Rt.

Figure 49 1880 O VAM 55 8/7 Checkmark

Figure 51 1880 O VAM 63 Medium O Set High

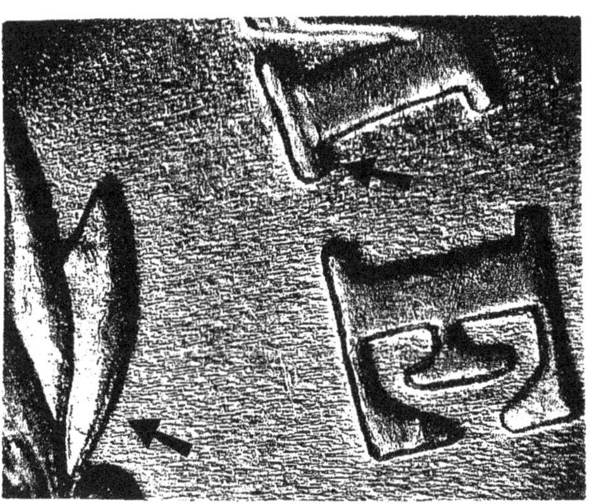

Figure 50 1880 O VAM 55 Doubled Rt. Reverse

VAM 6 combined with ***three*** other sub-varieties of different reverse dies of 6A with die gouge wreath, 6C & 6D with different clashed letters plus this obverse with ***two*** different reverse dies of VAMs 25 and 49 (formerly VAM 6B) and ***three*** weak 8/7 checkmarks of VAMs 16 shared with ***two*** VAMs 17 & 63, VAM 21 and the newly listed VAM 55. Thus, there are a total of **13** listed overdate die varieties for the 1880 O.

1880 S Overdates

The 1880 S overdate varieties are listed as 80/79, 8/7 or 0/9 as follows: VAMs 8, 9, 10, 11 and 12. VAMs 8, 9 and 10 were reported by Ted Clark in December 1968, March 1969 and February 1969 respectively. VAM 11 was reported by James Cornish in April 1967 and VAM 12 by Gordon Harnack in October 1972. They include some of the ***most controversial*** listed overdates in the Morgan series and all were refuted by Flynn except for VAM 12 which he calls a possible 8/7 overdate.

VAMs 8 and 9 8/7 Ear share the same obverse as shown in Figures 53 & 54 and has raised metal in most of the second 8 upper loop with a horizontal line at the bottom of this raised metal. A faint spike shows at the top left outside of this second 8 and the 0 shows a small raised area at the top right inside where it appears on some other 1880 overdates. VAM 8 has a medium S mint mark and VAM 9 has a large S mint mark that is doubled to the left of the top serif. They are both listed as Top 100 varieties but only have a modest premium. The 18-0 are all doubled at the very bottom as shown in Figures 52 & 53.

The controversy with VAMs 8 and 9 is that the raised metal within the 8 upper loop is a wider height than other 1880 overdates. Actually the 7 digit crossbar is as high as the 8 digit upper loop opening. The 8 over 7 photo overlay with the 7 in a low position under the 8 shows that most of the 8 upper loop is filled with the 7 crossbar. So if the 8 was punched in high over the 7 there is the possibility that the 7 crossbar remains would fill most of the 8 upper loop height if it didn't receive much die polishing. Nevertheless, the top left spike, horizontal line at bottom of 8 upper loop opening and raised metal at top right inside of 0 are all strong indicators present in ***other*** 1880 overdates and are too much of a ***coincidence*** in VAMs 8 and 9 not to call them overdates. Besides, if the 1880 P, CC and O minted coins all have numerous overdates, why wouldn't some of the S mint coins also show these modified overdate dies?

VAM 10 8/7 Crossbar shown in Figure 57 has a horizontal line across the bottom inside of the second 8 upper loop that curves slightly downward into a bar on early strike coin specimens. Early strike coins also show a horizontal raised metal area of thin bars and dots in the middle of the upper loop with raised metal also at the right inside. Flynn's excellent photos of an early die state VAM 10 also show raised dots where the left and right ears above the upper loop show on other 1880 overdates.There is no visible checkmark on the second 8 or raised metal within the 0. A marginal looking overdate, particularly in later die states, with ear dots missing and less raised metal in the upper part of 8 upper loop. But the horizontal line and rough raised metal in the upper loop and ear dots are in the ***right*** place for a low set 7 under the 8 as shown in the low 7 photo superposition. It remains a listed weak overdate. There is slight doubling of the bottom of the 1, top inside of the first 8 lower loop and lower left outside of the upper loop as shown in Figure 56. The reverse has doubled legend letters and slightly doubled wreath leaves shown in Figure 55. The large S mint mark is tilted left. Although a Top 100 coin, it only has a modest premium because of the weak evidence as an overdate.

VAM 12 8/7 Spikes shown in Figure 63 has many characteristics present in the 1880 overdates including a very visible checkmark and spike ear at top left of 8 upper loop. This ***alone*** is enough to label it an overdate but it also shows a faint vertical line at top right outside, a slight bulge at top right inside of upper loop and a faint diagonal pointed dash attached to the bottom outside of the lower loop. Also, the 0 has a small raised metal area at top right inside. This should be adequate evidence that VAM 12 is a weak overdate. The 1 is slightly doubled on the surface at the right side, the left 8 is doubled at the top left and right inside of the lower loop and the right 8 is slightly doubled at the lower left outside of the upper loop as shown in Figures 62 & 63.

Figure 52 1880 S VAM 8/9 Doubled 18

Figure 53 1880 S VAM 8/9 80/79 Ear, Doubled 0

Figure 54 1880 S VAM 8/9 80/79 Ear

Figure 55 1880 S VAM 10 Doubled Legend

Figure 56 1880 S VAM 10 Doubled 18

Figure 57 1880 S VAM 10 8/7 Crossbar

Figure 58 1880 S VAM 11 Doubled 18

Figure 59 1880 S VAM 11 0/9

Figure 60 1880 S VAM 11 0/9, Thread-Like Impression

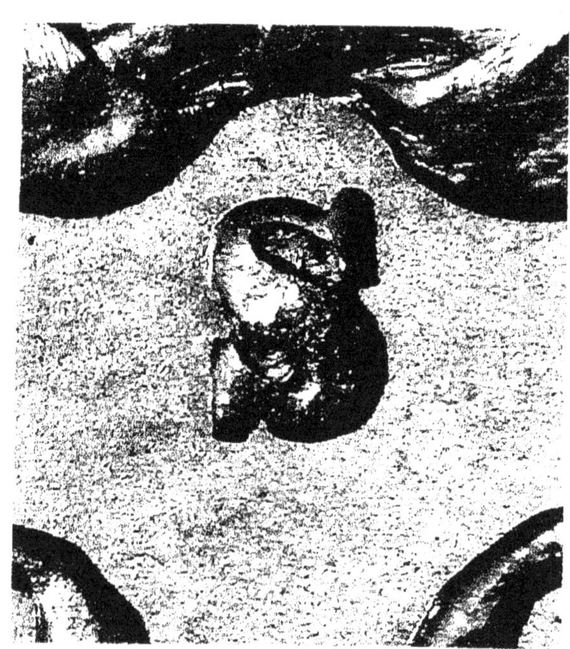

Figure 61 1880 S VAM 11 S/S

Figure 62 VAM 12 Doubled 18

Figure 63 1880 S VAM 12 8/7 Spikes, Checkmark

Figure 64 1880 S VAM 12
Die 1 Polishing Line n- G

Figure 65 1880 S VAM 12
Die 2 Doubled Arrow Head

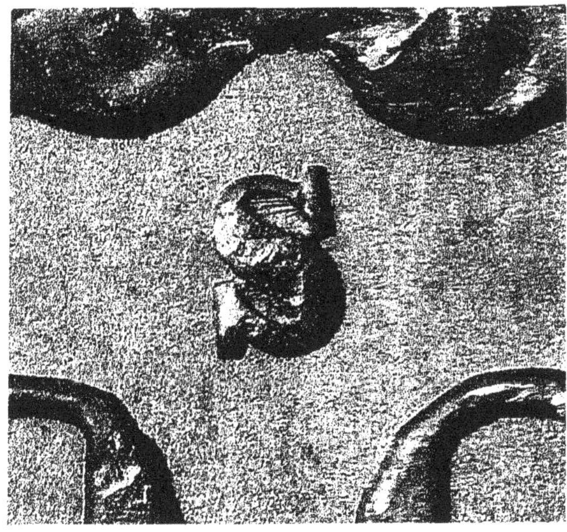

Figure 66 1880 S VAM 12
Die 1 S Mint Mark

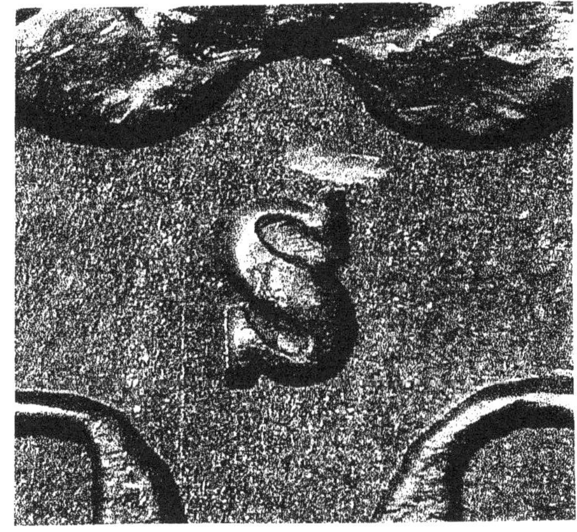

Figure 67 1880 S VAM 12
Die 2 S Mint Mark

There are two reverse dies with this VAM 12 obverse die. Reverse die 1 has the IV S mint mark at normal height with partially filled loops and polishing lines in the upper loop and slight tilt to left plus polishing line between n and G of In God as shown in Figures 64 & 66. Reverse die 2 has a IV S mint mark at normal height with partially filled loops and doubled lower edge of the bottom arrow head as shown in Figures 65 & 67.

VAM 11 0/9 overdate shown in Figure 59 is perhaps the ***most controversial*** of all the Morgan overdates as a first glance suggests that the raised metal within the 0 resembles somewhat the top of a 1! There is raised metal within the top of the 0 showing as a wide vertical area intersecting the top inside of the 0, straight lower right side and diagonal top left with a notch on top left. Heavy polishing lines are visible on the raised area. There is a bulge of the top left outside of the 0, just like many of the 1880 overdates, probably from the open die cavity of the bottom of the 9 upper loop.

Actually one of the ***convincing*** aspects of the raised metal within the 0 is the very visible ***notch*** at the upper left which is also present inside the 0 of the 1880 CC VAM 4 overdate. This is the junction of the 9 upper loop bottom outside with top right inside of the lower loop. The position of this notch or 9 loops junction would vary depending upon the position of the 9 under the 0.

To test this idea, scale 9 and 0 numerals about one inch high were carved into wooden blocks and impressed into modeling clay to simulate the punching of 0 over 9 digits in the metal die. A wax cast of the clay 0/9 depression was then prepared to show what might remain within the 0 on a coin without extensive die polishing. The wax cast shown in the previous simulation photo in the Overdate Simulation section of the 0 top inside shows the 9 upper loop lower right outside and upper part of 9 lower loop which closely matches the VAM 11 remains inside the 0 and also the 1880 CC VAM 4. The previous photo superposition with high 9 shows the same thing. Die polishing could have removed the lower part of the 9 lower loop within the 0. This should solidify the evidence that VAM 11 is an 0/9 overdate.

Ted Clark in his discussion of this variety in the *Collectors' Clearinghouse* article in *Coin World* November 18, 1970 issue summarizes his findings as follows:

> "Similar features to the 9 in the 1880/79 CC (VAM 4) and the same joining of the thicker extra metal in the 12 to 2 o'clock area like the three overdates mentioned above (CC VAM 4, S VAM 8, O VAM 4), combined with the strong bulge of the 0 as stated, is just TOO much of a coincidence for me not to call it 1880/9-S."

There is slight doubling of the 1 on the right side surface and the left inside of the first 8 lower loop as shown in Figure 58. A small hooked thread-like impression is on the Liberty head neck as shown in Figure 60. The S mint mark is doubled at the inside of both top and bottom loops as shown in Figure 61. Although listed as a Hot 50 variety, it only has a modest premium because of it's availability and the controversy of the remains within the 0.

The 1880 S has ***two*** fairly strong 80/79 of VAMs 8 and 9, ***two*** weak 8/7 of VAMs 10 and 12 and the ***one*** controversial 0/9 of VAM 11 for a total of **five** listed overdate die varieties.

Conclusions

1880 was a ***banner*** year for the Morgan dollar overdates!! They varied from being very bold, complete and obvious for the 1880 CC VAMs 4, 5 and 6 to the faint and subtle ones requiring careful examination. It is interesting to note that the first reported 1880 overdate was in 1964. The rest were reported in various years up through 1978. No additional overdates were reported for almost 30 years when Jeff Oxman reported a new 1880 O overdate of VAM 55 in February 2005. Since then, a new overdate die combinations has been added for each of the 1880 P & O, two overdate sub-varieties for each of the 1880 P & O and one overdate sub-variety for the 1880 CC.

- 1880 P VAMs 2 and 11 overdates are the same dies and VAM 2 should be eliminated or referred to as VAM 2/11 as VAM 11 had the more correct description and was reported first.
- 1880 P VAM 25 has too little evidence on the 0 to be called an 0/9 and should only be designated as a doubled date.
- 1880 P VAM 10 8/7 Bit is still listed as a possible overdate but the evidence isn't conclusive.

● 1880 CC VAM 10 has too little evidence to be called an overdate and should only be called a dash under the 8 and doubled 8.

● All of the other listed overdates should be retained and continue to stand the test of time from the early 1970s when Ted Clark studied and wrote extensively about most of them.

● 1880 P has ***four*** strong, ***one*** moderate, ***three*** weak, ***three*** die combinations or clashed die sub-varieties and ***one*** possible but not conclusive overdates for a total of **12** listed overdate varieties..

● 1880 CC has ***three*** strong and ***three*** weak overdates plus ***one*** clashed die sub-variety for a total of **seven** listed overdate varieties..

● 1880 O has ***three*** strong, ***five*** that share a strong obverse, ***three*** weak overdates that have ***two*** shared weak obverses for a total of **13** listed overdate varieties.

● 1880 S has ***two*** fairly strong, ***two*** weak overdates and ***one*** controversial 0/9 overdate for a total of **five** listed overdate varieties.

● The 1880 year of Morgan dollars has a total of 15 ***strong,*** three ***fairly strong to moderate*** and 17 ***weak*** overdates for a **grand total** of ***35 overdate*** listed die variety combinations. There are also two listed weak possible or controversial overdates. Collectors have much to look for in the 1880 year for the Morgan dollar overdate die varieties!

1882 O/S OVER MINT MARKS: REAL OR DIE BREAKS

The three 1882 O/S Morgan dollar over mint marks, VAMs 3, 4 & 5, have been known for over forty-five years. They have been widely accepted by collectors, dealers and the various grading services for all of those years and are all Top 100 varieties. However, all three were refuted by Kevin Flynn in his 1998 book, *Morgan Dollar Overdates, Over Mintmarks, Misplaced Dates, and Clashed E Reverses.* In the following paragraphs, each of the three so-called O/S mint marks will be examined to see if the O/S designation is supported. Photo superpositions are provided showing how the O over S mint marks should look. A three dimensional O/S simulation is shown using wooden carvings of the O and S mint marks impressed into clay to see if the coin evidence can be duplicated.

Historical Background

The 1882 O/S VAM 3 Flush and VAM 4 Depressed were first pictured by Francis Klaes in his 1963 pamphlet *Die Varieties of Morgan Silver Dollars.* VAM 3 was identified as a possible O over O and VAM 4 was identified as a possible O over S. VAM 5 was shown and listed as O over S Broken in Van Allen's December 1965 book *Morgan and Peace Dollar Varieties.* George Mallis in his June 1965 draft of a book *United States Silver Dollar Morgan Type* listed the early die state of VAM 3. Bill Fivaz reported the early die state of VAM 4 in October 1975 and Jim Baxter reported the early die state of VAM 5 in December 1976. The so-called O/S varieties have been known for over 45 years for the late die states and 30 to 40 years for the three early die states.

Die Variety Descriptions

Figure 68 shows a photo of the 1882 O **VAM 3** O/S Flush variety with the S diagonal shaft almost flush with the surrounding O mint mark. An early die state of VAM 3 is shown in Figure 69 with two raised diagonal ridges showing within the O. This shows that the initial punch of the O over the S forced metal into the S diagonal shaft cavity almost filling it up. As the die was used to strike coins, the pressures on the die during striking caused the metal in the diagonal shaft cavity to chip out.

VAM 3 has a doubled 82 with the second 8 slightly doubled at the lower left outside of the upper loop and the 2 is doubled at the right outside of the upper loop as shown in Figure 74.

All three O/S varieties show heavy polishing lines inside and below the Liberty head ear. VAM 3 has vertical lines in the ear as shown in Figure 77 whereas VAMs 4 & 5 have diagonal lines in the ear. There is also a clashed die state showing partial incuse us from the reverse Trust in the lower right hair vee as shown in Figure 78 listed as **VAM 3A.**

VAM 4 O/S Depressed or Recessed is shown in Figure 70 with the S diagonal shaft depressed or recessed below the O surface and slightly lower than VAM 3. An early die state of VAM 4 is shown in Figure 71 with a diagonal raised line and ridge within the O. Again this shows that the initial punch of the O over S almost completely filled the S diagonal shaft cavity. VAM 4 has a slightly doubled ear at the lower right inside, bottom outside and upper right outside. It also has a doubled 82 with second 8 doubled at left outside of both loops and the 2 at the right outside of the upper loop as shown in Figure 75.

VAM 5 O/S Broken is shown in Figure 72 with the S diagonal shaft flush with the O surface but only extending down from the left to the middle of the O opening. Only part of the S diagonal shaft chipped out with the die use. Figure 73 shows the early die state of VAM 5 with two diagonal lines and slightly raised metal at the left side of the O opening. VAM 5 also has a doubled 82 with the second 8 doubled on the left side of the upper loop and the 2 doubled at the top outside of the upper loop as shown in Figure 76.

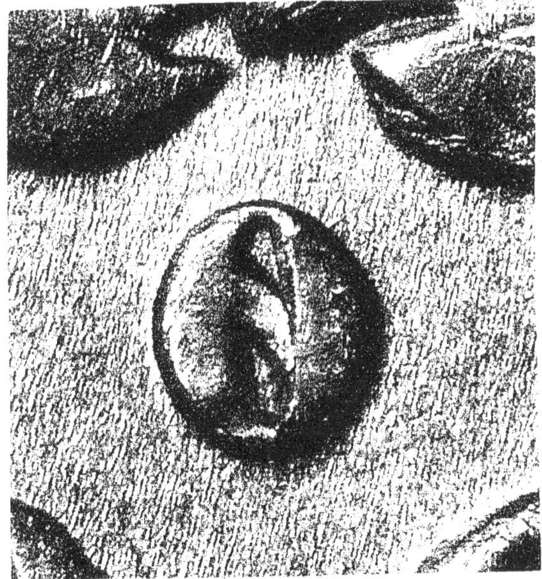

Figure 68 1882 O VAM 3 O/S Flush

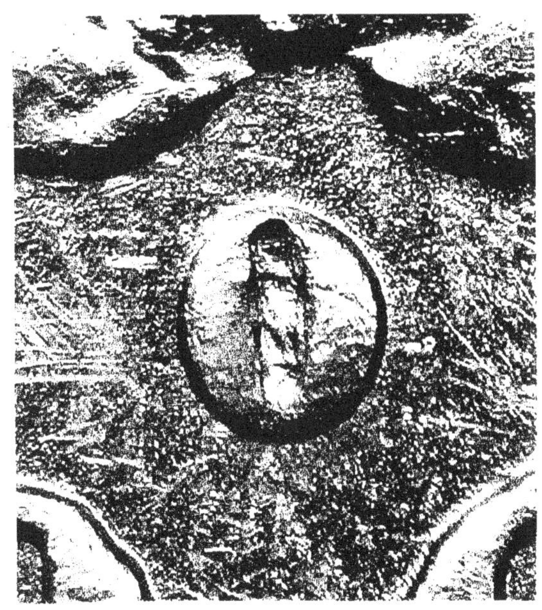

Figure 69 1882 O VAM 3 O/S EDS

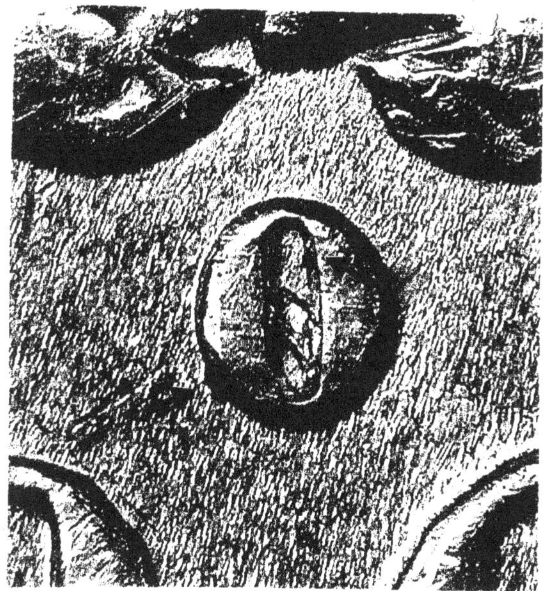

Figure 70 1882 O VAM 4 O/S Depressed

Figure 71 1882 O
VAM 4 O/S EDS

Figure 72 1882 O VAM 5 O/S Broken

Figure 73 1882 O
VAM 5 O/S EDS

Figure 74 1882 O VAM 3 Doubled 82

Figure 75 1882 O VAM 4 Doubled 82

Figure 76 1882 O VAM 5 Doubled 82

Figure 77 VAM 3 Lines in Ear

Figure 78 1882 O VAM 3A Clashed us

All three O/S varieties are fairly scarce and command significant premiums in price– especially in grades MS 62 and higher. The early die state of VAMs 3 and 5 are rare with the VAM 4 EDS being ultra-rare. All of the EDS varieties have more of a premium than the full O/S varieties because of their rarity.

S Mint Mark Shape

Flynn states that the curvature and width of the bar inside the three so-called O/S mint marks don't match the 1882 S mint mark he pictured. His photo doesn't exactly match the shape, width and curvature of the center shaft of most of the S mint marks on coins pictured in the 1992/98 VAM book editions. Many of the VAM book photos show a narrower width and more curve of the diagonal shaft. Figure 79 shows a photo of a typical medium S mint mark of 1880 S VAM 7 of the type used from 1879 through 1900 for the Morgan dollar. Figure 80 shows a photo of an 1883 O VAM 8 with tall oval O mint mark with narrow opening used from 1879 through 1884. The width of the S diagonal shaft would vary at the coin field level and letter top depending on the depth of the S punch in the die, strike strength to fill up the die cavity, basining and polishing of the die and coin wear. The width of the S diagonal shaft would always be narrowest at the deepest recesses in the working die.

The shape and curve of the diagonal shaft within the O would also vary depending on the lateral and rotational position of the O over the S. These weren't necessarily exactly centered as the over punch would have been done by the hand holding the punch and a mallet hitting it. So the curvature and width of the diagonal shaft inside the O mint mark matches many of the pictured S mint marks in the VAM book with the S mint mark set slightly left in some cases. Since the O mint mark completely surrounds the diagonal shaft of the S mint mark and has a narrow opening, a strong punch of the O into and deeper than the original S cavity would also tend to force metal into the diagonal shaft cavity of the S mint mark and make it narrower.

Figures 81, 82 & 83 show photo a superposition of the 1883 O VAM 8 O mint mark over the 1880 S VAM 7 S mint mark with the S centered, high and low. Note that the centered and low superposition show parts of the S lower serif at the lower left outside of the O.

Evidence of S Outside O

Flynn also states that there were no tops or bottoms of an S mint mark visible. However, for uncirculated coins, there is a ***vertical bar*** on the lower left outside of the VAM 4 O mint mark with a short vertical line connected to the field which is the remains of the left lower serif of the S mint mark as was shown in Figure 70. The top right inside of the O mint mark opening shows a short ***vertical line*** where the bottom of the upper loop of the S intersected the O. VAM 5 also shows in the same lower left outside area a weak line on the O side and in the adjacent field (See Figure 72.). VAM 3 doesn't show anything in this area. For the benefit of new collectors, the VAM 4 O/S with evidence of S outside the O was pictured in the November 3, 1976 *Collectors' Clearinghouse* page of *Coin World* in an article *Van Allen presents theory on overdates.* The amount of S showing outside the O would vary with the amount of die polishing.

Die Breaks?

Thirdly, Flynn asserts that "This variety is only the result of the die crack which progressed until a large chunk of metal fell out of the center". It is a ***strange coincidence*** that three dies in the same year would have ***very similar*** diagonal die break bars in the center of the O mint mark! Late die states of all three show ***smooth*** top surfaces and well defined smooth curves on the sides. No other date in the Morgan dollar series show this smooth top, raised diagonal bar within an O mint mark. It is also

Figure 79 1880 S VAM 7
S Example

Figure 80 1883 O VAM 8
O Example

Figure 81 O/S Centered S
Photo Superposition

Figure 82 O/S High S
Photo Superposition

Figure 83 O/S Low S
Photo Superposition

unlikely that purely random die chips would produce these smooth surfaces and curves! None of the VAMs 3, 4 & 5 O mint marks show die cracks on the outside of them.

Early die states of VAMs 3, 4 & 5 show ***progressive*** die chips flaking out of the O mint mark center until the late die states of bars is reached. What apparently happened was the punching of the O mint mark with narrow opening and wide sides caused the metal flow to fill most of the S diagonal shaft cavity. The top and bottom loops cavities of the S mint mark would have closely matched the top and bottom of the O mint mark as was shown in Figures 81, 82 & 83 photo superpositions. Under the tremendous pressure of the O mint mark punch with narrow opening, the displaced metal flowed into the S diagonal shaft die cavity narrowing and tending to fill it. Die polishing would further eliminate some of the remaining S evidence. The stress of striking coins on the die caused this displaced metal in the S diagonal bar cavity to later progressively chip out.

Test Punches Into Clay

To test the O over S mint mark theory, large 1 1/4 inch height wood carvings of the tall oval II O and medium IV S mint marks used in 1882 were prepared by tracing the photos of these mint marks on blocks of wood and carving away the surrounding wood as shown in Figure 84. These wood letter blocks were then impressed into modeling clay to simulate punching an O over S. Of course the modeling clay is not hard like die steel, but it should show similar plastic flow of material when the O block letter is impressed into the S cavity.

The accompanying pictures of Figures 85 and 87 show the O impressed shallow and deep over the S cavity in modeling clay. The resulting positive wax casts taken from the two clay molds simulate a struck coin as shown in Figures 86 and 88. They show remarkably ***similar*** bars inside the O to those of VAM 3 Flush and VAM 4 Depressed varieties. The diagonal bar became narrower than the wooden S model letter and the S serifs outside the O became smaller and shallower. These S serifs could have been polished off on the actual dies.

Conclusions

Readers can draw their own conclusions from the above evidence and answers to these questions:

- Can it be a mere coincidence that **three** working dies show a similar **smooth** top **diagonal** raised bar within the O mint mark on this one 1882 date?
- Would **random** die chipping produce a **smooth** raised surface diagonal bar with smooth curved sides?
- Do the diagonal bars closely **resemble** that of the medium S mint mark diagonal shaft, keeping in mind that the punched oval O mint mark with narrow opening would likely displace the original S mint mark diagonal cavity shape in the die somewhat?
- Is there **evidence** of the S serif on the lower left **outside** of the O mint mark?
- Did the punching of wood carvings of an O and S mint mark letters into modeling clay result in wax casts that look similar to VAMs 3 and 4?
- Should the 1882 O VAMs 3, 4 & 5 O/S designations be retained? I vote **YES**! Collectors, coin dealers and grading services continue to recognize and attribute these three varieties as O/S.

Figure 84 S & O Letters Wooden Blocks

Figure 85 O/S Clay Impressions
Flush Letters

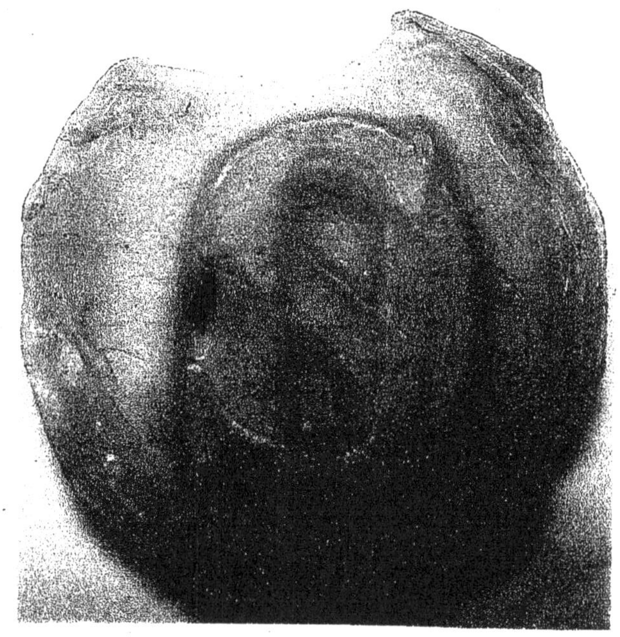

Figure 86 O/S Wax Cast Flush

Figure 87 O/S Clay Impressions
Depressed S

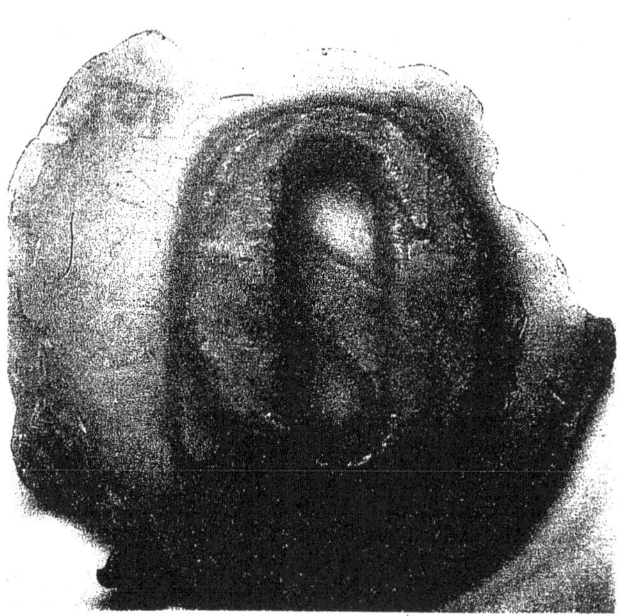

Figure 88 O/S Wax Cast Depressed S

MORGAN DOLLAR 1887 OVERDATES

There are two known overdate die varieties for the 1887 Morgan dollar; one for 1887 P and one for the 1887 O. They are designated as VAM 2 7/6 and VAM 3 7/6 overdates respectively and are both Top 100 varieties. The 1887 P VAM 2 7/6 overdate was reported by Walter Breen in October 1972 and the 1887 O VAM 3 7/6 overdate was reported by Bob Reithe in February 1973. These two overdates have long been accepted in the numismatic community as collectable overdates because of their strong evidence.

The 1887 P VAM 2 7/6 is fairly scarce in all grades and is available in proof-like condition. It commands a sizeable premium in all grades. The 1887 O VAM 3 7/6 is scarcer than the 1887 P VAM 2 7/6 and commands an even larger premium, especially in MS 63 and 64, the highest grades available. It is exceedingly rare in proof-like condition.

Figure 89 shows the **1887 P VAM 2** 7/6 with a long curved line extending up from the lower right side and a short wide spike or bar on the lower left side. A short vertical spike shows at the very top of the crossbar.

Figure 90 shows the **1887 O VAM 3** 7/6 also with a long curved line extending up from the right bottom and a short line on the lower left side. There is no evidence of the underlying 6 at the top of the 7.

The underlying 6 is at slightly different positions on these two die varieties, with 1887 O 6 being lower than that on the 1887 P. Photo superpositions of the 7 over 6 digits are shown in Figures 93 and 94 with a centered 6 and high 6 respectively. The 6 is a photo of the 1886 Proof VAM 15 example and the 7 is an 1887 P VAM 13 example shown in Figures 91 and 92 respectively. The photo superpositions illustrate where the bottom loop of the 6 would show on either side of the lower part of the 7 shaft. The high 6 position matches closely the 1887 P VAM 2 6 position underlying the 7 with short spike at the top of the 7 crossbar from the inner left edge of the 6 upper loop.

The 6 and 7 date digits were also carved into the end of wooden blocks as shown in Figure 95. These were pressed into modeling clay to simulate the three dimensional punching of these digits into steel working dies. Figure 96 shows the clay mold with the 6 and 7 pressed at the same depth and Figure 97 shows the 7 deeper than the 6. Wax casts of these clay molds are shown in Figures 98 and 99. The wooden digits pressing into clay with the 7 deeper than the 6 closely simulates the actual 7/6 overdates. Die polishing after the 7 was punched over the 6 would have removed much of the underlying 6.

Figure 89 1887 P VAM 2 7/6

Figure 90 1887 O VAM 3 7/6

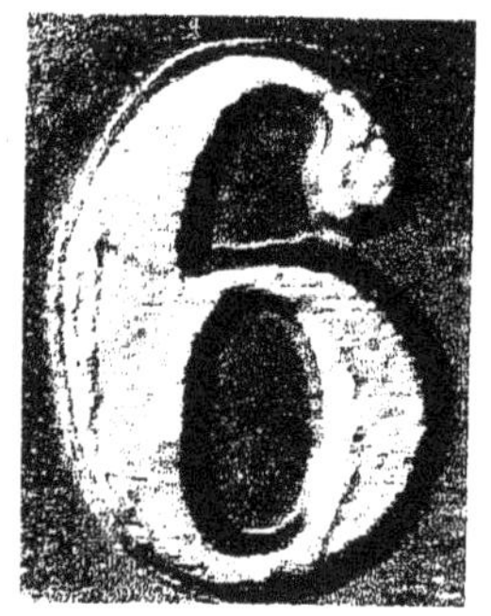

Figure 91 1886 Proof VAM 15
6 Example

Figure 92 1887 P VAM 13
7 Example

Figure 93 7/6 Centered
Photo Superposition

Figure 94 7/6 High
Photo Superposition

Figure 95 6 and 7 Wooden Date Digits

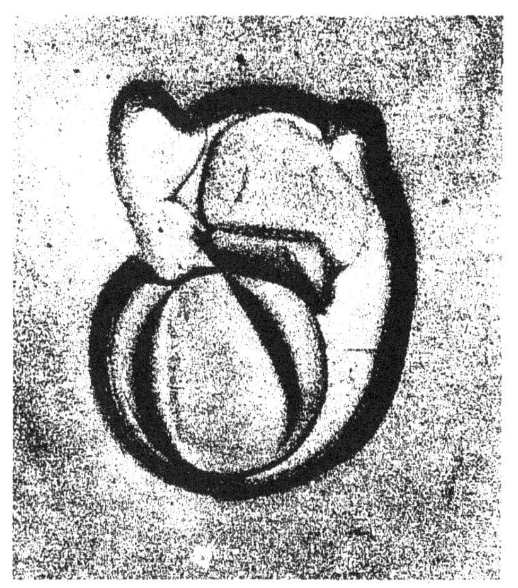

Figure 96 7/6 Clay Mold 6 & 7 Same Depth

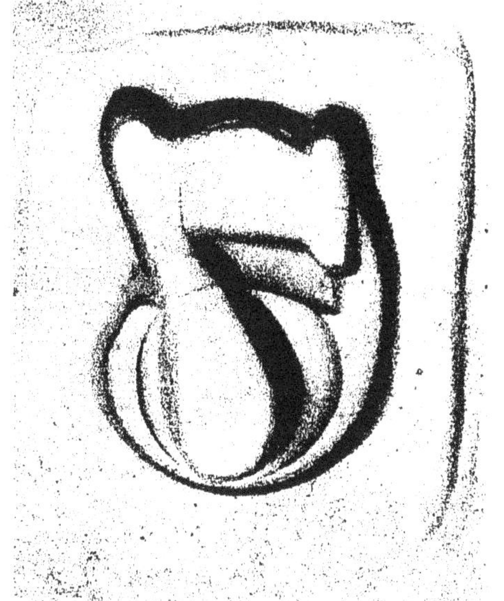

Figure 97 7/6 Clay Mold 7 Deeper Than 6

Figure 98 7/6 Wax Cast 6 & 7 Same Depth

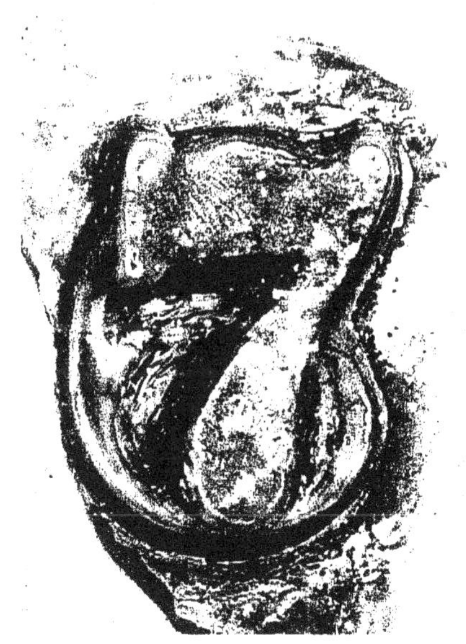

Figure 99 7/6 Wax Cast 7 Deeper Than 6

1900 O/CC OVER MINT MARKS

There are five primary 1900 O with O/CC over mint marks: VAMs 7/10, 8, 9, 11 & 12. They show varying amounts of the underlying CC mint mark in slightly different positions. They are all listed as Top 100 varieties. VAMs 10, 8, 11 & 12 are somewhat available in all grades including the higher mint state grades and command substantial premiums. VAMs 7 & 9, however, are very scarce and are rare in BU, so they have a much larger premium price. Very few of the 1900 O/CC occur in BU proof-like condition.

There are several sub-varieties of the O/CC varieties. The scarce VAM 7A has a small die chip above the 9. VAM 8 has a later die state, VAM 8A, that has rust pits around the O/CC mint mark. A even later die state shows clashed dies, VAM 8B, with the rust spots and a clashed letter n next to Liberty head neck and st in the lower right hair vee. VAM 10A also has a later die clash state with clashed n on obverse and a raised M on reverse.

Historical Background

VAMs 7 and 12 were first shown in Francis Klaes 1963 pamphlet *Die Varieties of Morgan Silver Dollars.* VAM 7A was reported by Jim Hart in September 1999. VAMs 8, 8A, 9 & 11 were reported by the author in December 1965 in the book *Morgan and Peace Dollar Varieties.* VAM 10 was reported by Martin Field in September 1979, VAM 8B by Mark Kimpton in March 2005 and VAM 10A by Ash Harrison in June 2003.

The Carson City Mint stopped striking silver dollars in 1893 with a low mintage of only 677,000. Undoubtedly some die pairs sent to the Carson City Mint for use in 1893 were never used in the coining presses. The unused reverse dies could be used at other branch mints by punching a different letter of O or S and polishing the dies to remove most of the underlying CC mint mark. They couldn't be used at the Philadelphia Mint, which didn't have a mint mark on Morgan dollars, because of the difficulty in removing all of the CC remains. But why did a delay of seven years occur before these over mint marks were used at the New Orleans Mint?

There was a financial panic in 1893. Mine production of silver on the Comstock had fallen off and the San Francisco Mint could handle all of the western mines output. With the repeal of the Sherman Act in 1893 that authorized the striking of silver dollars, the Treasury Department did not require coinage of large amounts of silver dollars at that time. On June 1, 1893 the Carson City Mint was ordered to suspend coining operations and have only its refining department remain open. In 1895 it was found that gold was missing at the Carson City Mint and the refinery operations were suspended. Three mint employees were convicted in 1896 of stealing the gold and the refinery operations reopened again on June 9, 1896. The higher coining costs of the Carson City Mint compared to the San Francisco Mint, the missing gold bullion scandal of 1895 and the fact that the San Francisco Mint could handle all of the western mines silver output all contributed to the closing of the Carson City Mint facility in 1899.

An article appeared in the *Coin World Collectors' Clearinghouse* in the March 18, 1964 issue titled *Taxay Backs Up Theory About O Over CC Dollar.* James Johnson, editor, had sent an example coin of the 1900 O/CC to Don Taxay (Who had written several books on minting subjects.) and asked for an explanation if the O/CC really existed. The article states:

> "Taxay verified the coin and backed up our theory indirectly by saying that when inspectors visited the Carson City Mint several years after it closed, they found the dies there and took them back to Philadelphia. That would explain why the CC dies were available for use seven years after the Carson City Mint was finished."

The closing of the Carson City Mint is documented in the book *Mint Mark "CC"* by Howard Hickson, 1972, published by The Nevada State Museum.

Page 73 states: "...even though the Carson City facility was legally a mint, it had been a mere assay office with refinery facilities since 1893."
Page 75 states: "In 1899... the mint $15,000 financing bill... passed and the Treasurer, Secretary quickly issued an edict stating that mint would become an assay office on July 1." It is doubtful that the dies would have been removed before the Carson City Mint was officially closed in 1899.
Page 97 states: "After the coining department closed in 1893, the machine (The First Coin Press) stood idle in the pressroom until it was dismantled and shipped to the Philadelphia Mint in 1899... By the middle of September, 1899, the mint had been stripped of most of the mint machinery: the last press was taken apart for packing."

Coinage of the Morgan dollar was much higher at the New Orleans branch mint than the San Francisco Mint in 1900 (Over 12 million vs 3.5 million.). To supply the New Orleans Mint with working dies for this heavy coinage (Even higher than the Philadelphia Mint coinage of 8.8 million silver dollars.), the left over Carson City Mint reverse dies were modified by punching the O mint mark over the CC mint mark and polished to eliminate much of the underlying CC letters.

Die Variety Descriptions

The **VAM 7** O//CC Low shown in Figure 100 is the weakest of the underlying CC of the five known O/CC varieties. The O is centered over the CC with only the curved lines at the left and right at the bottom of the O. VAM 7 also has a slightly doubled first 0 at the bottom left outside with the date in the normal position as shown in Figure 101.

A sub-variety **VAM 7A** has a small die chip at the top of the 9 in the date for the late die state as shown in Figure 112.

VAM 10 has the same reverse as VAM 7 but with a different obverse die. It has a near date set further left than normal with the left edge of the 1 bottom crossbar over the second denticle space to the right of the neck point (As pictured and discussed on page 115 in the VAM book.). There is no doubling on the date digits. Later die states of VAM 10 show clashed dies of **VAM 10A** sub-variety with a faint incuse n of In from the reverse next to the Liberty head neck as shown in Figure 114. It also has a faint raised designer's initial M from the obverse showing above d in God.

VAM 8 O/O/CC Centered Shifted Left shows the O centered over the CC with a slight shift of the CC to the left as shown in Figure 102. It is actually an O/O/CC as the O is doubled at the top left side. Two thick spikes of a C show on the right upper and bottom of the O and a thin curved line is on the left side of the O. The middle and late die states of the VAM 8 show progressive die chipping to expose more of the remains of the doubled O (See Figures 103 & 104.). VAM 8 also has a near date without any doubling on the date digits.

VAM 8A shown in Figure 105 has some raised dots around the O/CC mint mark from a rusted die. There are some die polishing lines around the eagle's left leg that are identical for VAMs 8 and 8A shown in Figures 106 and 107 indicating that they are the same dies. This was discussed in detail in the May 1978 issue of the *Numismatic Error Collectors of America* monthly *Errorscope* magazine which is presented at the end of this section.

VAM 8B has clashed dies with a partial n of In next to the Liberty head neck shown in Figure 113. It also has a partial incuse st of Trust from the reverse showing in the right hair vee of the lower hair edge. The raised dots around the O/CC mint mark are still present of VAM 8A.

VAM 9 O/CC Centered Shifted Right is shown in Figure 108 and is very scarce. It shows the underlying CC centered but shifted slightly to the right. There is a short detached thick spike at the lower right outside of the O and a curved line with visible C serif at the top right outside. The left outside of the O shows a faint broken curved line. The obverse has the date set further left than normal with doubling at the top inside of the 900 digits (See Figure 109.). The ***key*** to identifying VAM 9 is the doubled 900 and the short thick but **detached** spike at the lower right outside of the O mint mark.

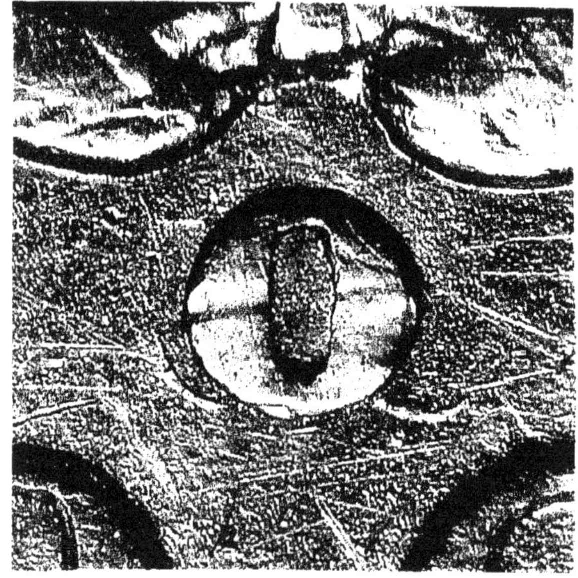

Figure 100 1900 O VAM 7 & 10 O/CC Low

Figure 101 1900 O VAM 7 Doubled First 0

Figure 102 1900 O VAM 8 O/O/CC Centered, Shifted Left

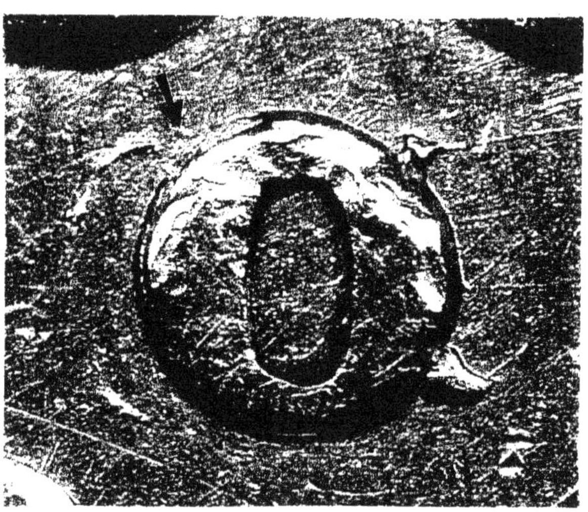

Figure 103 1900 O VAM 8 Middle Die State

Figure 104 1900 O VAM 8 Late Die State

Figure 105 1900 O VAM 8A O/O/CC Centered, Shifted Left, Rust Spots

Figure 106 1900 O VAM 8 Die Polishing Lines

Figure 107 1900 O VAM 8A Die Polishing Lines

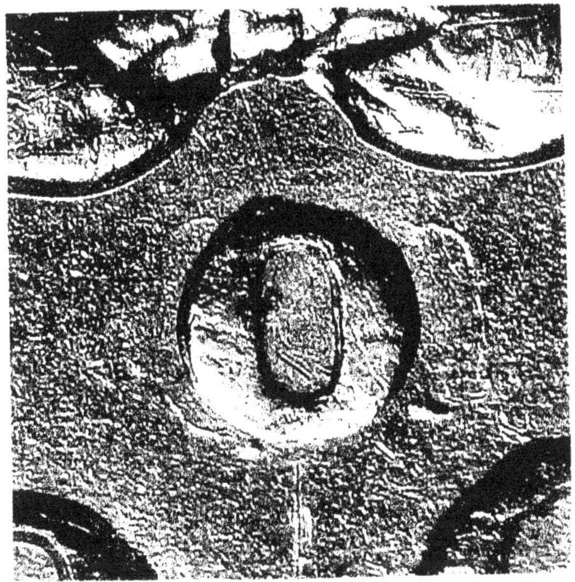

Figure 108 1900 O VAM 9 O/CC Centered, Shifted Rt.

Figure 109 1900 O VAM 9 Doubled 900

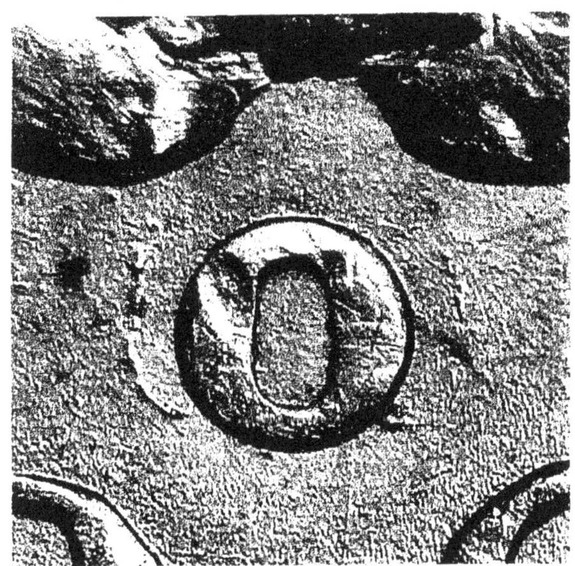

Figure 110 1900 O VAM 11 O/CC High, Shifted Left

Figure 111 1900 O VAM 12 O/CC High, Shifted Rt.

VAM 11 O/CC High Shifted Left is shown in Figure 110 and has the underlying CC set high with a little shift to the left. There is a short thick spike next to the lower left outside of the O, a faint C serif at top right outside and a thick curved line at the left outside. The obverse has a very near date without any die doubling.

VAM 12 O/CC High Shifted Right is shown in Figure 111 and has the most complete underlying CC of any of the five O/CC varieties with the CC set high and slightly to the right. The lower curve of the right C shows at the lower right outside of the O and there is a thick spike with the C serif at the top right of the O. A complete thin curved line with top serif of the left C shows close to the left outside of the O. The obverse has a near date without any die doubling.

The Changing Mint Mark-- 1900 O/CC VAM 8

The 1900 O/CC VAMs 8 and 8A are fascinating because of the way their appearance changes with die state. The progressive die chipping of the mint mark area can be followed from early to the late die states. It is one of the few dies of the Morgan dollar series in which the mint mark changes, besides the three 1882 O/S dies. In addition, Kevin Flynn in his 1998 book *Morgan Dollar Overdates, Over Mintmarks, Misplaced Dates, and Clashed E Reverses* claims that VAMs 8 and 8A obverse and reverse dies have different die markers with different location and thickness of mint marks and are not the same varieties. However, an article by yours truly in the May 1978 issue of the Numismatic Error Collectors of America (now part of CONECA) monthly *Errorscope* magazine, entitled *"THE CHANGING MINT MARK– 1900 O/CC UPDATE"* showed that the then listings of VAMs 8 and old 10 (now 8A) were the same dies. For the benefit of recent collectors who haven't seen that article, it's repeated below as it is still timely today.

THE CHANGING MINT MARK– 1900 O/CC UPDATE

By Leroy C. Van Allen

Denny Thostenson's fine article on the 1900 O/CC in the February 1978 issue of the Errorscope posed the contention that the VAM's 8 and 10 were of the same die. After studying BU and circ. specimens of each variety, I am in complete agreement with Denny that VAM's 8 and 10 are different states of the same die. I'll point out this evidence in the following paragraphs....

To begin with, both VAM's 8 and 10 have the same obverse with a near date... The diagonal polishing marks in the hairline above the date are also the same although VAM 10 is weaker because of more advance die wear. Some VAM 8's show the beginnings of a fine die crack from the left of the upper serif of the 1 which is much more pronounced on the VAM 10's. Another point which will be important in explaining the reverse is that none of the VAM 8's I've seen have die clash marks whereas all VAM 10's do.

VAM's 8 and 10 had been listed separately in the (1976) VAM book because there were no intermediate die states between their reverses showing the die chips or rust spots at various stages. Either the reverse die field was clear as in VAM 8 or spotted as in VAM 10. Also, the O's have different appearances between VAM's 8 and 10.

There are characteristic marks on the reverse of both VAM 8 and 10 that show they are indeed the same die. There are diagonal polishing marks just above the arrow shafts between the tail feathers and the eagle's left leg feathers. Also, by turning the coins so that AMERICA is upright, there is a line of die chips between the eagle's left leg and the leg feathers.

Of course, the tip-off is that the CC under the O has identical shape and placement on both VAM 8 and 10. The 10 CC are somewhat obliterated by die chips or mint marks.

A complicating factor is that the appearance of the O mint mark changes on the VAM8's so that the early die state VAM 8 O's look very much different than the VAM 10's. It has been pointed out in *Coin World's Collectors' Clearinghouse* and by others that VAM 8 is actually an O/O/CC. On the early die state VAM 8 with proof-like surface there is just a fine line on the left and top outside of the O, and as a fine curved line at the bottom inside. As the die was used, portions of this doubling of the O became stronger and more raised above the field.

What happened is that the O was originally punched to the NW of the final O. Since the O was punched over the CC, the metal flowing into the original O cavity by the final O had been displaced at least three times– first by the CC mint mark punch, second by the original O, and third by the final O. Apparently this weakened the metal in this area and as the die was used, die chips kept falling out of the original O cavity until it was almost completely re-exposed!

So, in the early die state VAM 8 with P/L surfaces, there are just fine lines outlining the original O outside and inside the final O. Then die chips strengthen the doubling at the top outside and a projection at the lower right inside appears. The die chipping next progresses to strengthen and raise the doubling on the left outside with just a narrow gap between the top and side doubling. The VAM 10's show almost all of the NW doubling completely raised with the doubling at the bottom inside completely raised from the die chip removal process.

VAM 10 reverse is obviously a later die state than VAM 8 because of this die chipping process on the doubled mint mark. Backing this up are heavy die cracks through the legend letters on VAM 10 but none or very weak ones on VAM 8. Also, VAM 10 shows clashed dies on all obverses and some of the reverses. One explanation for the die chips or rust spots on the field of the VAM 10 and not the VAM 8 could be based on this die clash. Presumably, the dies received heavy die clashes and were set aside for a few weeks or months. Rust could have developed on the field around the mint mark during this time. The dies were then reused in the press, the clash marks rediscovered on the coins, the reverse clash marks stoned out, and then the dies reused until retirement. Because of the heavy reverse die cracks on VAM 10, the die could not have been used very much longer however.

At any rate, the coin evidence speaks for itself. VAM's 8 and 10 are different states of the same die. In addition, they are both O/O/CC with changing appearance of the O/O over the die lifetime. Also, the die suddenly picks up rust spots on the field around the mint mark late in it's life. Quite an interesting and changing variety! ...The VAM 10 is now assigned VAM 8A....

Figure 112 1900 O VAM 7A Die Chip Above 9

Figure 113 1900 O VAM 8B Clashed n

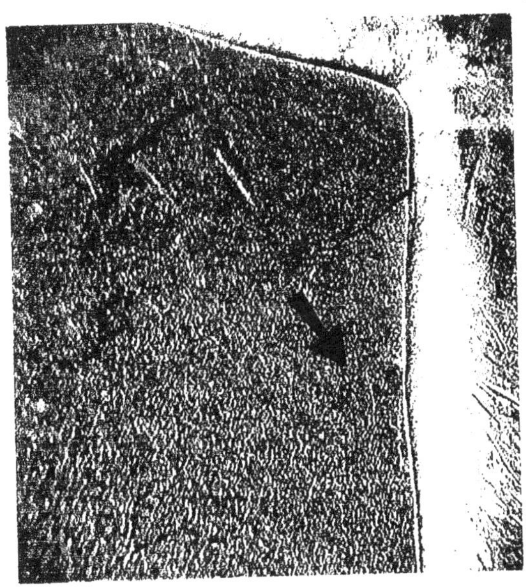

Figure 114 1900 O VAM 10A Clashed n

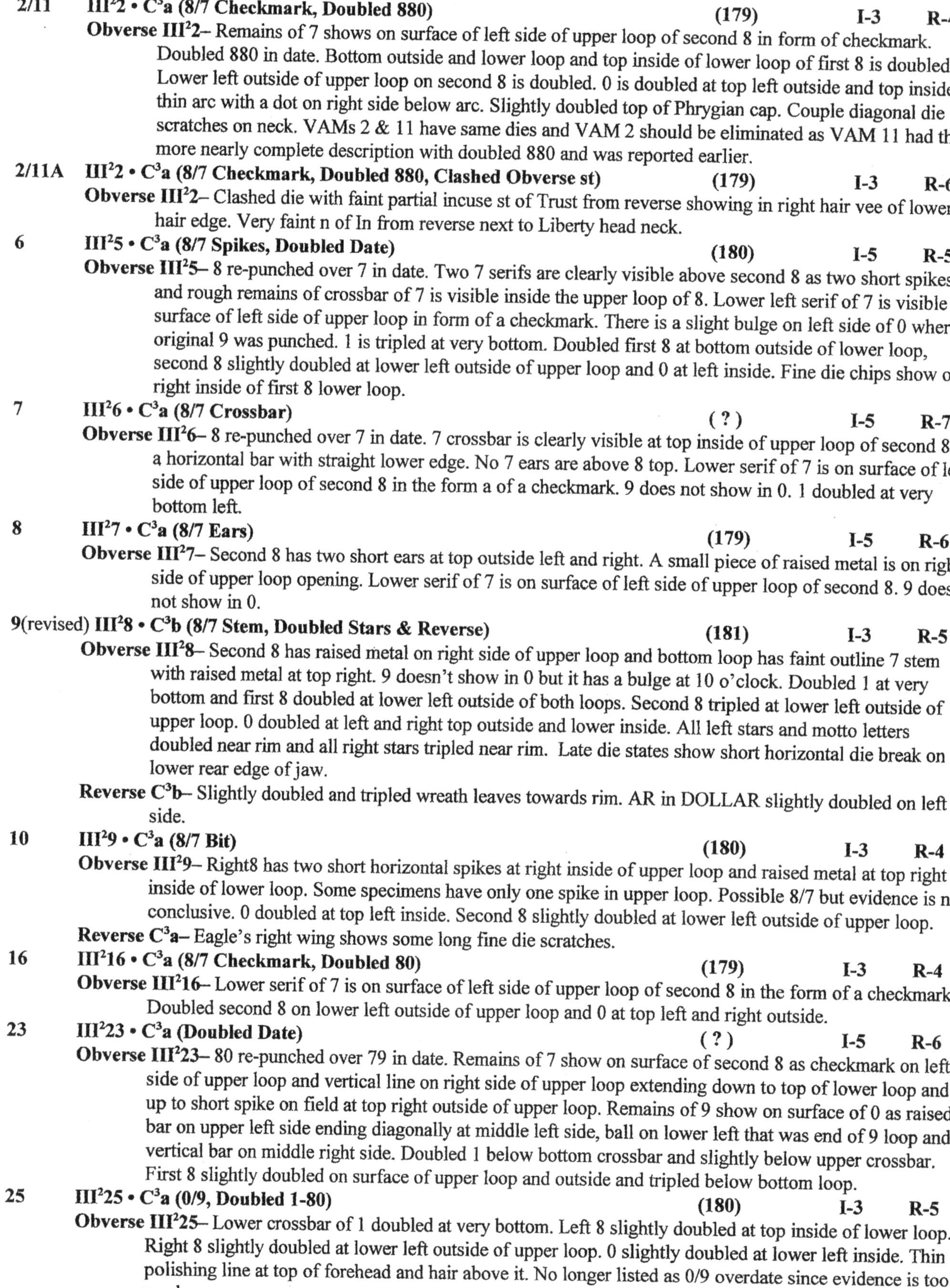

APPENDIX– VARIETY LISTINGS DESCRIPTIONS

1880 P

2/11 **III^{2}2 • C^{3}a (8/7 Checkmark, Doubled 880)** (179) I-3 R-4

Obverse III^{2}2– Remains of 7 shows on surface of left side of upper loop of second 8 in form of checkmark. Doubled 880 in date. Bottom outside and lower loop and top inside of lower loop of first 8 is doubled. Lower left outside of upper loop on second 8 is doubled. 0 is doubled at top left outside and top inside as thin arc with a dot on right side below arc. Slightly doubled top of Phrygian cap. Couple diagonal die scratches on neck. VAMs 2 & 11 have same dies and VAM 2 should be eliminated as VAM 11 had the more nearly complete description with doubled 880 and was reported earlier.

2/11A **III^{2}2 • C^{3}a (8/7 Checkmark, Doubled 880, Clashed Obverse st)** (179) I-3 R-6

Obverse III^{2}2– Clashed die with faint partial incuse st of Trust from reverse showing in right hair vee of lower hair edge. Very faint n of In from reverse next to Liberty head neck.

6 **III^{2}5 • C^{3}a (8/7 Spikes, Doubled Date)** (180) I-5 R-5

Obverse III^{2}5– 8 re-punched over 7 in date. Two 7 serifs are clearly visible above second 8 as two short spikes and rough remains of crossbar of 7 is visible inside the upper loop of 8. Lower left serif of 7 is visible on surface of left side of upper loop in form of a checkmark. There is a slight bulge on left side of 0 where original 9 was punched. 1 is tripled at very bottom. Doubled first 8 at bottom outside of lower loop, second 8 slightly doubled at lower left outside of upper loop and 0 at left inside. Fine die chips show on right inside of first 8 lower loop.

7 **III^{2}6 • C^{3}a (8/7 Crossbar)** (?) I-5 R-7

Obverse III^{2}6– 8 re-punched over 7 in date. 7 crossbar is clearly visible at top inside of upper loop of second 8 as a horizontal bar with straight lower edge. No 7 ears are above 8 top. Lower serif of 7 is on surface of left side of upper loop of second 8 in the form a of a checkmark. 9 does not show in 0. 1 doubled at very bottom left.

8 **III^{2}7 • C^{3}a (8/7 Ears)** (179) I-5 R-6

Obverse III^{2}7– Second 8 has two short ears at top outside left and right. A small piece of raised metal is on right side of upper loop opening. Lower serif of 7 is on surface of left side of upper loop of second 8. 9 does not show in 0.

9(revised) **III^{2}8 • C^{3}b (8/7 Stem, Doubled Stars & Reverse)** (181) I-3 R-5

Obverse III^{2}8– Second 8 has raised metal on right side of upper loop and bottom loop has faint outline 7 stem with raised metal at top right. 9 doesn't show in 0 but it has a bulge at 10 o'clock. Doubled 1 at very bottom and first 8 doubled at lower left outside of both loops. Second 8 tripled at lower left outside of upper loop. 0 doubled at left and right top outside and lower inside. All left stars and motto letters doubled near rim and all right stars tripled near rim. Late die states show short horizontal die break on lower rear edge of jaw.

Reverse C^{3}b– Slightly doubled and tripled wreath leaves towards rim. AR in DOLLAR slightly doubled on left side.

10 **III^{2}9 • C^{3}a (8/7 Bit)** (180) I-3 R-4

Obverse III^{2}9– Right8 has two short horizontal spikes at right inside of upper loop and raised metal at top right inside of lower loop. Some specimens have only one spike in upper loop. Possible 8/7 but evidence is not conclusive. 0 doubled at top left inside. Second 8 slightly doubled at lower left outside of upper loop.

Reverse C^{3}a– Eagle's right wing shows some long fine die scratches.

16 **III^{2}16 • C^{3}a (8/7 Checkmark, Doubled 80)** (179) I-3 R-4

Obverse III^{2}16– Lower serif of 7 is on surface of left side of upper loop of second 8 in the form of a checkmark. Doubled second 8 on lower left outside of upper loop and 0 at top left and right outside.

23 **III^{2}23 • C^{3}a (Doubled Date)** (?) I-5 R-6

Obverse III^{2}23– 80 re-punched over 79 in date. Remains of 7 show on surface of second 8 as checkmark on left side of upper loop and vertical line on right side of upper loop extending down to top of lower loop and up to short spike on field at top right outside of upper loop. Remains of 9 show on surface of 0 as raised bar on upper left side ending diagonally at middle left side, ball on lower left that was end of 9 loop and vertical bar on middle right side. Doubled 1 below bottom crossbar and slightly below upper crossbar. First 8 slightly doubled on surface of upper loop and outside and tripled below bottom loop.

25 **III^{2}25 • C^{3}a (0/9, Doubled 1-80)** (180) I-3 R-5

Obverse III^{2}25– Lower crossbar of 1 doubled at very bottom. Left 8 slightly doubled at top inside of lower loop. Right 8 slightly doubled at lower left outside of upper loop. 0 slightly doubled at lower left inside. Thin polishing line at top of forehead and hair above it. No longer listed as 0/9 overdate since evidence is too weak.

Reverse C^{3}a– Three tiny die chips together in middle of eagle's right wing.

29 **III^{2}29 • C^{3}a (8/7 Checkmark, Doubled 80)** (178) I-3 R-4

Obverse III^{2}29– Lower serif of 7 is on surface of left side of upper loop of second 8 in the form of a checkmark. Right side of checkmark is more curved than VAM 16. Doubled second 8 on lower left outside of upper loop and 0 at top left and right outside, but not as strong as VAM 16. First 8 has die chip on upper left inside of lower loop.

Reverse C^{3}a– Some specimens show short die gouge between G & o in God.

29A **III^{2}29 • C^{3}a (8/7 Checkmark, Doubled 80, Clashed Obverse n)** (178) I-3 R-5

Obverse III^{2}29– Clashed die with partial n of In from reverse showing next to Liberty head neck.

53 **III^{2}29 • C^{3}f (8/7 Checkmark, Doubled 80, AMERICA & Rt. Wreath)** (179) I-3 R-5

Obverse III^{2}29– Clashed die of VAM 29A with partial incuse n showing at Liberty head neck.

Reverse C^{3}f– Slightly doubled AMERICA letters at bottom inside and top inside of DOLLAR letters towards rim. Right wreath outside leaves slightly doubled towards rim. *Die marker–* Diagonal die scratch in top cluster of right wreath.

1880 CC

4 **III^{2}3 • B^{2}a (80/79, Parallel Arrow Feathers Reverse)** (178) I-5 R-4

Obverse III^{2}3– 80 re-punched over 79 in date. Two serifs of 7 show above top of 8 left and right, horizontal crossbar at top inside of upper loop and stem on right side of lower loop. Lower serif of 7 is on surface of left side of upper loop as a checkmark. 9 shows within 0 as curved bar in upper left, straight vertical bar at upper right and small curved bar with polishing lines in lower half. A slight bulge shows at 10 o'clock outside on 0. 1 has die chip at top right of shaft. First 8 has vertical polishing lines inside partially filled loops.

5 **III^{2}4 • C^{3}c (8/7 High, Doubled 88)** (177) I-5 R-4

Obverse III^{2}4– 8 re-punched over 7 in date with original 7 punched high. Prominent ears show above 8, crossbar in upper loop, stem on right side of lower loop, dash below bottom of 8 and lower serif of 7 on surface of left side of upper loop as a checkmark. First 8 doubled at top inside of lower loop. Second 8 tripled at lower left outside of upper loop. Tops of U-U-UNUM doubled towards rim. Short die gouge from right side of first U in UNUM.

Reverse C^{3}c– Normal die of C^3 type with slanted arrow feathers and small II CC mint mark with slight tilt to right. Vertical die gouge between arrow feathers and olive branch.

6 **III^{2}5 • C^{3}d (8/7 Low)** (177) I-5 R-4

Obverse III^{2}4– 8 re-punched over 7 in date with original 7 punched low. Faint ears above 8 with 7 crossbar in middle of upper loop, stem at right inside of lower loop, dash well below bottom loop and lower serif of 7 on surface of left side of upper loop as a checkmark. Small piece of raised metal with polishing marks at bottom inside of 0. First 8 has diagonal polishing lines inside partially filled loops.

Reverse C^{3}d– Normal die of C^3 type with slanted arrow feathers and centered small I CC mint mark with dot in center of each C. Die scratches thru M in AMERICA, bottom of eagle's right wing and inside of eagle's left wing.

7 **III^{2}6 • B^{2}a (8/7 Dash, Parallel Arrow Feathers Reverse)** (177) I-3 R-4

Obverse III^{2}6– 8 re-punched over 7 in date. Short ear at top left, two diagonal polishing lines and die chips on right side and top inside of lower loop and dash below lower loop. Slight bulge at 10 o'clock on 0. First 8 is doubled at top inside of lower loop and has die chips inside upper loop. Slight doubling on nose and chin plus top edge of Phrygian cap.

7A **III^{2}6 • B^{2}a (8/7 Dash, Clashed Obverse n)** (177) I-2 R-5

Obverse III^{2}6– Clashed die with faint partial incuse n of In from reverse next to Liberty head neck.

8 **III^{2}6 • C^{3}d (8/7 Dash, Small CC)** (177) I-3 R-3

Obverse III^{2}6– Same die as VAM 7 but has been polished after receiving heavy clash marks. A vertical die polishing line shows on right outside between loops of second 8.

9 **III^{2}6 • C^{3}a (8/7 Dash, Large CC)** (?) I-3 R-5

Reverse C^{3}a– Normal die of C^3 type with large V CC mint mark and slanted arrow feathers.

1880 O

4 **III^{2}3 • C^{3}a (80/79, Doubled 188, Micro O)** (176) I-4 R-4

Obverse III^{2}3– 80 re-punched over 79 in date. Faint ears at top left and right above 8, partial horizontal crossbar at right inside of upper loop and lower serif of 7 on surface of left side of upper loop as a checkmark. 0 has raised metal at top right inside. Doubled 1 on right side of vertical shaft and first 8 on left inside and right outside of lower loop. Second 8 doubled at left outside of both loops.

5 **III^{2}4 • C^{3}b (8/7 Ear, Oval O)** (176) I-4 R-5

Obverse III^{2}4– 8 re-punched over 7 in date. Almost complete horizontal bar within second 8 upper loop and faint ear at top left outside. Very faint lower serif of 7 on surface of left side of upper loop as a checkmark. No raised metal in 0.

Reverse C³b– Die scratch below wreath center, within mint mark opening, below arrow shaft and spike from eagle's left wing to neck. Medium tall II O oval mint mark.

6 **III²5 • C³a (8/7 Spike, Micro O)** (176) I-4 R-5

Obverse III²5– 8 re-punched over 7 in date. A long spike extends from top left outside of second 8. Small horizontal spike on right inside of upper loop of second 8 and a checkmark from the remains of the 7 lower serif show on surface of left side of upper loop. Doubled profile and top of Phrygian cap.

Reverse C³a– Micro I O mint mark.

6A **III²5 • C³a (8/7 Spike, Clashed Obverse st, Reverse M)** (176) I-4 R-5

Obverse III²5– Clashed die with partial incuse st of Trust from reverse showing in right hair vee of lower hair edge. Faint tick of n next to neck from In of reverse.

Reverse C³a– Faint raised designer's initial M from obverse above d in God. Die gouge on left side of left wreath.

6B/49 (See VAM 49)

6C **III²5 • C³a (8/7 Spike, Clashed Obverse In, We, ust, Reverse M)** (176) I-5 R-6

Obverse III²5– Strongly clashed die with partial incuse In of In from reverse next to Liberty head neck, partial incuse ust of Trust from reverse showing in right hair vee of lower hair edge, and partial incuse We of We from reverse in space between hair locks at right of designer's initial M. Later die state than VAMs 6A & 6B/49.

Reverse C³a– Strongly clashed die with raised designer's initial M from obverse showing above d in God. Later die state than VAMs 6A and 6B/49.

6D **III²5 • C³a (8/7 Spike, Clashed Obverse st)** (?) I-4 R-5

Reverse C³a– Non-clashed die with single clashed obverse st & faint n of VAM 6A and 6B/49. No die gouge in left wreath of VAM 6A or hangnail die gouge in tail feathers of VAM 6B. Early die state of VAM 6C before multiple clashing. *Die markers–* Thin two segment die crack between top right of o and top left of d in God. Horizontal die scratch on left most top leaf of leaf cluster next to bow in left wreath.

16 **III²13 • C³o (8/7 Check Mark, Micro O Set Right)** (176) I-3 R-5

Obverse III²13– 8 re-punched over 7 in date. Remains of 7 lower serif shows on surface of left side of upper loop of second 8 in form of a check mark. Short vertical bar on surface at right side of junction of 8 loops extending down into side of top of lower loop opening. Second 8 doubled on lower left outside of upper loop.

Reverse C³o– Die 1– Small micro I O mint mark set slightly to right with slight tilt to right. Die 2– Centered small micro I O mint mark.

17 **III²13 • C³b (8/7 Checkmark, Medium O)** (176) I-3 R-5

21 **III²16 • C³a (8/7 Checkmark, Ear, Doubled 880, Motto, Alligator Eye)** (176) I-3 R-5

Obverse III²16– 8 re-punched over 7 in date. Lower serif of 7 on surface of left side of right 8 upper loop as a checkmark set high. Vertical line on side of lower loop opening at upper right. Faint short ear at top right outside of upper loop. Doubled 880. Slightly doubled left 8 at top and right inside of lower loop, right 8 at lower left outside of upper loop and 0 at lower left inside. E PLURIBUS UNUM doubled strongly at top of letters and 7 left star and 4-6 right stars doubled towards rim. Slightly doubled hair front, LIBERTY band front and upper nose profile. Die scratch on eye front giving appearance of alligator eye.

Reverse C³a– Slightly doubling of A-F-AMERI and top leaf cluster of right wreath towards rim.

61 (Eliminated, same as VAM 21.)

25 **III²5 • C³g (8/7 Spike, High Micro O Set Right)** (176) I-4 R-5

Obverse III²5– Same 8/7 Spike as VAM 6.

Reverse C³g– Small micro I O mint mark set high and to right.

49 (formerly 6B)**III²5 • C³l (8/7 Spike, Hangnail Eagle, Doubled UNITED, Clashed Obverse n & st)** (176) I-4 R-6

Obverse III²5– Same die as VAM 6A but later die state with same clashed die partial incuse n of In from reverse next to Liberty head neck and partial incuse st of Trust from reverse showing in right hair vee of lower hair edge.

Reverse C³l– Same die gouge thru eagle's left tail feather and lower arrow feather as VAM 1A/48 with small micro I O mint mark.

55 **III²40 • C³p (8/7 Checkmark, Doubled Right Reverse)** (176) I-3 R-5

Obverse III²40– 8 re-punched over 7 in date. Remains of 7 lower serif shows on surface of left side of upper loop of second 8 in form of a check mark. Second 8 doubled at lower left outside of upper loop.

Reverse C³p– ATES OF AMER slightly doubled towards rim. In God We Trust doubled at top. Outside leaves of right wreath doubled on rim side. Centered small micro I O mint mark.

63 **III²13 • C³r (8/7 Check Mark, Medium O Mint Mark Set High)** (?) I-3 R-6

Reverse C³r– II O oval mint mark centered and upright set high. Some die polishing lines inside and slightly doubled on left inside.

1880 S

8 **III^{2}5 • C^{3}a (80/79 Ear, Doubled 18-0, Medium S)** **(186)** **I-4** **R-4**

Obverse III^{2}5– 80 re-punched over 79 in date. Second 8 has raised metal that fills lower three-quarters of upper loop with faint line at bottom inside of upper loop plus a faint spike at top left outside. 0 has small raised metal at top right inside and bulge at 10 o'clock outside. 18-0 in date slightly doubled with 1 at bottom of lower crossbar, left 8 at bottom right of lower loop and 0 at lower left inside and outside.

Reverse C^{3}a– Couple doubled leaves in left wreath.

9 **III^{2}5 • C^{3}e (80/79 Ear, Large S/S Top)** **(185)** **I-4** **R-4**

Reverse C^{3}e– Very large VI S mint mark re-punched with original showing as a spike to left of top serif.

10 **III^{2}6 • C^{3}q (8/7 Crossbar, Doubled 188 & Reverse Legend)** **(186)** **I- 4** **R-6**

Obverse III^{2}6– 8 re-punched over 7 in date. Second 8 has a few small dots at top within upper loop. Horizontal line shows at bottom of upper loop curving slightly up on left side. Raised metal on right inside of upper loop. No raised metal inside 0. Doubled 188 with 1 doubled at top left and very bottom. First 8 slightly doubled at top inside of lower loop and second 8 at lower left outside of upper loop.

Reverse C^{3}q– All legend letters doubled slightly in radial direction. Motto letters doubled at top. Right and left wreath doubled slightly towards rim. Very large centered VI S mint mark tilted left.

11 **III^{2}7 • C^{3}f (0/9, Medium S/S, Double 188)** **(184)** **I-4** **R-4**

Obverse III^{2}7– Raised metal at top and right inside of 0 with straight left side and hook at top left and polishing lines. Bulge at 10 o'clock outside. Top loop of second 8 has a few dots on right inside with a bulge at top right outside of lower loop. Doubled 1 on surface at right side of shaft and below upper crossbar. First 8 slightly doubled at left inside of lower loop. Second 8 doubled on lower left outside of upper loop. Slight slant to date. Small hooked struck thru thread-like impression at front of neck.

Reverse C^{3}f– Medium IV S mint mark set high and re-punched with short vertical spike extending downwards from middle of top loop opening and curved line in middle inside of lower loop opening.

12 **III^{2}8 • C^{3}d (8/7 Spikes, Doubled 188)** **(183)** **I-4** **R-4**

Obverse III^{2}8– 80 re-punched over 79 in date. Second 8 has a remains of 7 lower serif at left side of upper loop in form of a checkmark, a thin diagonal line at top left outside, a faint vertical line at top right outside, slight bulge of metal at top right inside of upper loop, diagonal pointed dash attached to bottom outside of lower loop and is doubled at bottom left outside of upper loop. 0 has small raised metal at top right inside and a slight bulge at top left outside. 1 is doubled slightly on surface at right side. First 8 doubled at top left inside and on right inside on surface of lower loop..Second 8 doubled on lower left outside of upper loop.

Reverse C^{3}a– Die 1– IV S mint mark at normal height with very slight tilt to left and partially filled loops with heavy polishing lines in upper loop. Very slightly doubled outside leaves towards rim in left wreath and some leaves in right wreath. Long polishing line from top of wing up between n and G of In God.
Die 2– IV S mint mark at normal height with partially filled loops. Slightly doubled middle leaves on left side in second and third leaf cluster from top of left wreath and couple doubled leaves in lower right wreath. Doubled lower edge of bottom arrow head and lower edge of eagle's left wing.

1882 O

3 **III^{2}3 • C^{3}b (O/S Flush, Doubled 82)** **(181)** **I-5** **R-4**

Obverse III^{2}3– Doubled second 8 on lower left outside of upper loop and bottom outside of lower loop. 2 doubled on right outside of upper lop. Polishing lines inside ear with area around neck over polished.

Reverse C^{3}b– O punched over S with diagonal bar of S center shaft flush within O. Small dots of metal all over eagle probably due to rusted die. A scarce earlier die state shows a thin diagonal line inside O.

3A **III^{2}3 • C^{3}b (O/S Flush, Clashed Obverse us)** **(181)** **I-5** **R-6**

Obverse III^{2}3– Clashed die with partial us of Trust from reverse showing in right hair vee of lower hair edge.

4 **III^{2}4 • C^{3}c (O/S Depressed, Doubled 82)** **(181)** **I-5** **R-3**

Obverse III^{2}3– Doubled second 8 on upper left outside of both loops and 2 at top right outside. Ear slightly doubled at lower right inside, bottom outside, and upper right outside with polishing lines inside. Small dots all over Liberty head from rusted die.

Reverse C^{3}c– O punched over S with diagonal bar of S center shaft depressed or recessed within O. Small dots of metal all over eagle probably due to rusted die. A rare earlier die state shows a diagonal tear drop at lower part of opening.

5 **III^{2}5 • C^{3}d (O/S Broken, Doubled 82)** **(181)** **I-5** **R-3**

Obverse III^{2}5– Doubled second 8 on upper left outside of upper loop and 2 at top outside. Polishing lines inside ear.

Reverse C^{3}d– O punched over S with partial diagonal bar of S center shaft at left side of O opening. Small dots of metal all over eagle probably due to rusted die. A scarce earlier die state shows a triangular dot at left side of O opening and as a fine line in middle.

1887 P

2 **III^{2}2 • C^{3}a (7/6)** **(189)** **I-5** **R-4**

Obverse III^{2}2– 7 re-punched over 6 in date. Bottom loop of 6 shows as a long curved line starting up from lower right bottom of 7 and extending upwards one-third of digit height. A short thick spike shows on left side of 7 shaft that slants upwards at one-third way up of shaft. Short vertical spike shows at very top of 7 crossbar in the middle. A short spike also slants upwards from middle right side of crossbar.

1887 O

3 **III^{2}3 • C^{3}a (7/6)** **(181)** **I-5** **R-4**

Obverse III^{2}3– 7 re-punched over 6 in date. Bottom loop of 6 shows as a long curved line starting from lower right bottom of 7 and extending upwards almost one-half of digit height. Left side of 7 shaft shows a short spike that curves to left and up at a point one-third way up on shaft height.

Reverse C^{3}a– Some specimens show a depression in eagle's breast due to a weak strike.

1900 O

7 **III^{2}4 • C^{3}e (O/CC Low, Doubled 0)** **(181)** **I-4** **R-7**

Obverse III^{2}4– First 0 in date slightly doubled at bottom left outside.

Reverse C^{3}e– Centered and upright O mint mark punched over CC. A curved line shows at lower right outside of O and a curved broken line shows at left outside.

7A **III^{2}4 • C^{3}e (O/CC Low, Die Chip Above 9)** **(181)** **I-4** **R-7**

Obverse III^{2}4– Small die chip at top of 9 in date.

8 **III^{2}5 • C^{3}f (O/O/CC Centered, Shifted Left, Near Date)** **(181)** **I-5** **R-4/5**

Reverse C^{3}f – Centered and upright O mint mark punched over CC. Early die state shows O doubled at top left outside with notch missing at 11 o'clock in doubling and doubled at bottom inside of opening as a thin curved line. Later die states show progressive die chipping at top left outside of O to reveal more of underlying O. Underlying CC is shifted slightly to left with thick spikes connected to right side of O at top and bottom and curved line shows at left outside.

8A **III^{2}5 • C^{3}f (O/O/CC Centered, Shifted Left with Rust Spots, Near Date)** **(189)** **I-5** **R-6**

Reverse C^{3}f – Die rust spots evident around mint mark area.

8B **III^{2}5 • C^{3}f (O/O/CC Centered, Shifted Left Rust Spots, Near Date, Clashed Obv n, st) (189)** **I-5** **R-5**

Obverse III^{2}5– Strongly clashed die with partial incuse n of In from reverse next to Liberty head neck and partial st of Trust from reverse showing in right hair vee of lower hair edge.

9 **III^{2}6 • C^{3}g (O/CC Centered, Shifted Right, Doubled 900, Slanted Near Date) (181)** **I-5** **R-7**

Obverse III^{2}6– Doubled 900 in date. Doubled 9 at top inside of upper loop and both 0's at top inside. Date set further left than normal and slanted with 0's higher than 1.

Reverse C^{3}g– Centered and upright O mint mark punched over CC. Underlying CC is shifted to right with thick spike detached from lower right outside of O and curved line with serif at top right outside. A broken curved line shows at left outside of O.

10 **III^{2}5 • C^{3}e (O/CC Low, Near Date)** **(181)** **I-4** **R-4/5**

10A **III^{2}5 • C^{3}e (O/CC Low, Near Date, Clashed Obverse n, Reverse M)** **(181)** **I-4** **R-5**

Obverse III^{2}5– Clashed die with faint partial incuse n of In from reverse next to Liberty head neck.

Reverse C^{3}e– Clashed die with faint raised designer's initial M from obverse showing above d in God.

11(revised) **III^{2}3 • C^{3}i (O/CC High, Shifted Left, Very Near Date)** **(181)** **I-2** **R-4/5**

Obverse III^{2}3– Very Near date at right edge of lateral position. Long thread-like impression above cap ribbon on some specimens. *Die marker*– Single diagonal polishing line below I in PLURIBUS.

Reverse C^{3}i– Centered and upright O mint mark punched over CC. Underlying CC is set slightly high and shifted to left with thick spike and curved line at lower right outside of O, faint serif at top right outside and thick curved line at left outside.

12 **III^{2}5 • C^{3}j (O/CC High, Shifted Right, Near Date)** **(181)** **I-5** **R-4/5**

Reverse C^{3}j – Centered and upright O mint mark punched over CC. Underlying CC is set high and shifted slightly to right with thick spike and curved line at lower right outside and thick spike with a serif at top right outside. A curved line with serif at top is at left outside of O. Heavy horizontal polishing lines around wreath bow area. Strongest appearing of five O/CC varieties.

FURTHER REFERENCES

Please check Amazon Kindle for Michael S. Fey, Ph.D., and Leroy Van Allen & A. George Mallis publications. For hard copy print of books, please contact Dr. Fey at RCI, P.O. Box C, Ironia, NJ 07845 or eMail: Feyms@aol.com.

Hard copy books are also available at *The Institute for Silver Dollar Education and Research*, at website: *Ilovesilver dollars.org* or by contacting Executive Director John Baumgart at John.Baumgart@comcast.net

Amazon Kindle

Fey, Michael S. 2019. *The Complete Virtual Guide to Pricing Your Morgan Silver Dollars*. 286 pp. RCI

Van Allen, Leroy, & A. George Mallis. 2023. *Part I or II or III of Three. Comprehensive Catalog and Encyclopedia or Morgan & Peace Dollars*. RCI Total 520 pp.

Leroy Van Allen. 2011. *Wonders of Morgan Dollars*. 139 pp. RCI

Leroy Van Allen. 2013. *Wonders of Peace Dollars*. 273 pp. RCI

Leroy Van Allen. 2006. *Morgan Dollars 8 & 7 Over 8 Tail Feather Story*. 52 pp. RCI

Leroy Van Allen. 2010. *1878 P 7 Tail Feather Morgan Dollar Attribution Guide*. 130 pp. RCI

Leroy Van Allen. 2006. *1878 S Morgan Dollar Attribution Guide*. 139 pp. RCI

Fey, Michael S. 2009 The Top 100 Morgan Dollar Varieties: The VAM Keys

FURTHER REFERENCES

Hard Copy Books

Fey, Michael S. 2019. The Top 100 Morgan Dollar Varieties: The VAM Keys. 286 pp. RCI

Fey, Michael S. 2008. *A Decade of Top 100 Insights.* RCI 174 pp.

Van Allen, Leroy. 1991. *RotaFlip Die Rotation Booklet and Guide.* 1991. RCI

Kimpton, M.D., Mark. 2005. *Elite Clashed Morgan Dollars.* RCI 160 pp

Van Allen, Leroy, & A. George Mallis. 2023. *Comprehensive Catalog and Encyclopedia or Morgan & Peace Dollars.* RCI Total 520 pp.

Van Allen, Leroy 2011. *Wonders of Morgan Dollars.* 139 pp. RCI

Van Allen, Leroy 2013. *Wonders of Peace Dollars.* 273 pp. RCI

Van Allen, Leroy 2006. *Morgan Dollars 8 & 7 Over 8 Tail Feather Story.* 52 pp. RCI

Van Allen, Leroy 2010. *1878 P 7 Tail Feather Morgan Dollar Attribution Guide.* 130 pp. RCI

Van Allen, Leroy 2006. *1878 S Morgan Dollar Attribution Guide.* 139 pp. RCI

Van Allen, Leroy 2013. *Die Gouges and Scratches Peace Dollar Attribution Guide. 109 pp* RCI

Van Allen, Leroy 2008. *1921 Scribbles Morgan Dollar Attribution Guide.* 234 pp. RCI

Van Allen, Leroy. 2013. *Misplaced Date Digits Morgan Dollar Attribution Guide.* 57 pp RCI

Van Allen, Leroy. 2017. *Dashed Under 8 Morgan Dollar Attribution Guide.* 53 pp. RCI

Van Allen, Leroy. 2009. *Overdates and Over Mint Marks of Morgan Dollar Attribution Guide.* 53 pp. RCI

Van Allen, Leroy. 2015. *Denticle & Die Impressions Morgan Dollar Attribution Guide.* 109 pp. RCI

Van Allen, Leroy. 2009. *1921 P Infrequently Reeded or Wide Reeding Morgan Dollar Attribution Guide.* 31 pp. RCI

Van Allen, Leroy. 2011 *Amazing Changing 1921 S VAM 1B Thorn Head Morgan Dollar.* 2011. 22 pp. RCI

Van Allen, Leroy. 2009. *1889 P Doubled Ear Morgan Dollar Attribution Guide.* 32 pp. RCI

Van Allen, Leroy. 2016. *Micro o and Other Counterfeit Morgan and Peace Dollars.* 191 pp RCI

Van Allen, Leroy. 2005. *Micro o Mint Mark on Morgan Dollars.* 32 pp. RCI

Van Allen, Leroy. 2005. *Die Markers for 1921 Morgan and Peace Proof Dollars.* 9 pp. RCI

Van Allen, Leroy and Baumgart, John. 1992-Date Various VAM Book Yearly Supplements. RCI

www.ingramcontent.com/pod-product-compliance
Ingram Content Group UK Ltd.
Pitfield, Milton Keynes, MK11 3LW, UK
UKHW062000290726
14090UKWH00021B/1306

9 798991 964869